The Divine Romance

Experiencing Intimacy with God

Debra White Smith

BEACON HILL PRESS
OF KANSAS CITY

Copyright 2009
By Debra White Smith and Beacon Hill Press of Kansas City

ISBN 978-0-8341-2443-1

Printed in the
United States of America

Cover Design: Arthur Cherry
Interior Design: Sharon Page

Library of Congress Cataloging-in-Publication Data
Smith, Debra White.
The divine romance : experiencing intimacy with God / Debra White Smith.
    p. cm.
Includes bibliographical references.
ISBN 978-0-8341-2443-1 (pbk.)
1. Spiritiuality. 2. Spiritiual life—Christianity. 3. Prayer—Christianity. I. Title.
BV4501.3.S645 2009
248.4—dc22

                                                                        2009012503

10 9 8 7 6 5 4 3 2 1

CONTENTS

PREFACE

Dear friend,

Before I became an author and speaker, I had been developing a divine romance for years. It was through this process of sitting in the presence of God and laying my concerns before Him that some of my bestselling titles have been birthed. In this book I'm sharing the prayer concepts that I live by and the great power that is available to the people of God when they commit time to listening to and communicating with their holy Creator.

This book will lead you down the path that has already revolutionized my life and brought about miraculous healing and deliverance in the lives of both me and my husband. But be warned! The path to revolutionary prayer is not quick or cheap. It will cost your time, your effort, and your willingness to relinquish everything you are—your very will—to the control and direction of a holy God. It will cost your eyesight—because He will ask you to exchange your eyes for His and view your life and world as He views them. It will cost your hearing—because He will ask you to train your ears to hear His voice above all else. And it will cost your past, your present, and your future—because if you let Him, He will heal your past, empower your present, and plan your future.

The divine romance is not a journey that is always easy; but it is always exciting! There is no greater life than praying with faith and seeing your prayers answered one after another. There is no greater experience than regularly stepping into the holy of holies and being immersed in the presence of a God who empowers and anoints. There is no greater existence than seeking God's face just because He is the great I Am.

He is the same I Am whom Moses encountered in the burning bush. Moses was going about his normal duties pasturing flocks in the mountains when he encountered that burning bush. God met him where he was. He even told Moses to take off his sandals, because he was standing on holy ground.

When I Am came in the form of man and stretched himself out on the Cross, He did so to meet us where we are. But we have to take the time to encounter Him and give Him the time to ignite the blaze within our souls. God is ready and waiting right where we are. Are you ready to take off your shoes and step onto holy ground?

Joining you in the journey,
Debra White Smith

1
The Sandals

❦❧

"Do not come any closer," God said.
"Take off your sandals, for the place
where you are standing is
holy ground" *(Exodus 3:5).*

I stumbled into the divine romance as a young mother. I'll never forget where it started: the side of my bathtub behind a locked bathroom door. It was the only place I could find some reprieve from my energized toddler. Leaving him to the care of my husband, I simply plopped myself onto the side of the bathtub and said, "God, I really want to see you move in my life."

I would love to tell you that I had visions of shining angels or that God's voice boomed from behind the shower curtain. But nothing so grandiose happened. So many times our journey with God happens just like that—in the ordinary. My father recently told me, "We would really be in trouble if God met us only Sunday in church. But He meets us every day in all kinds of situations. I don't know how many miles I've driven, crying so hard I could hardly see, because God's presence was so strong." As God met Moses on the job and my dad behind the wheel of a truck, so He met me, a young woman who was hungry for Him. So I simply listened for the voice of God within my heart and began the quiet journey of romancing the Lord.

I had been in the church my whole life, spent several years as a pastor's child, and had been taught all the stories of God's miraculous power. I knew all the terminology, doctrine, and theology. I was a devout Christian who did everything in my power to please the Lord and to live a holy life.

I had held all sorts of offices in the church and enjoyed this service to the King. Yet still I knew there must be more.

In my heart I began to think, *If all this stuff in the Bible is really true, then I want to see God's activity in my life on a powerful level as well.* So I simply asked God to start moving in my life. I am living proof that anytime someone simply sits and waits on God, He will move in a mighty way. I have come to firmly believe that God is waiting on us to recognize His holiness for what it is—to the point that we fall silent and ask Him to reveal himself on a deeper level.

The story of Moses' encounter with the burning bush is so typical of the way God desires to encounter us. Scripture states that Moses was taking care of business as usual. He was on the job, tending his father-in-law's flock when

The angel of the LORD appeared to him in a blazing fire from the midst of a bush; and he looked, and behold, the bush was burning with fire, yet the bush was not consumed. So Moses said, "I must turn aside now and see this marvelous sight, why the bush is not burned up." When the LORD saw that he turned aside to look, God called to him from the midst of the bush and said, "Moses, Moses!" And he said, "Here I am." Then He said, "Do not come near here; remove your sandals from your feet, for the place on which you are standing is holy ground." He said also, "I am the God of your father, the God of Abraham, the God of Isaac, and the God of Jacob." Then Moses hid his face, for he was afraid to look at God. . . . Then Moses said to God, "Behold, I am going to the sons of Israel, and I will say to them, 'The God of your fathers has sent me to you.' Now they may say to me, 'What is His name?' What shall I say to them?" God said to Moses, "I AM WHO I AM"; and He said, "Thus you shall say to the sons of Israel, 'I AM has sent me to you'" *(Exodus 3:2-6, 13-14, NASB).*

Anyone who is familiar with the area Moses was in will tell you that burning bushes are not uncommon. The desert gets so hot and the terrain is so dry that certain bushes spontaneously combust. A man of the desert, Moses would have known this. But what was different about this bush was that it was burning and not being consumed by the fire. This unique situation caught Moses' attention to the point that he went to investigate. The most pivotal part of this whole story is that only when Moses turned aside did God speak to him.

The story of the burning bush holds so many images that are reality in our lives. As Christians, we hold a precious marvel that is just as miraculous as the burning bush—Jesus Christ. Born of a virgin, He became the living sacrifice for our sins. Most Old Testament scholars agree that when the angel of the Lord appears in Scripture, He is the pre-incarnate Christ (Jesus before His conception as a human being). Just as the fire in the bush needed no fuel to maintain its flame, so the sinless Son of God was not bound by normal methods of procreation when He was conceived in a virgin's womb. So the flame that needed no fuel is a symbolic representation for the God-Man, Jesus, who existed before humans were even formed.

Most Christians will readily say they want God to speak to them. They even long to hear His voice. But many times we fail to take the time to do what Moses did—turn aside to look upon the holy presence of a holy God. Only when we take those steps toward God and pause will He speak to us. According to Sandra D. Wilson, "In our relationship with God, the problem isn't that he doesn't speak; it's that we are often unwilling to listen."[1] Oswald Chambers agrees: "Why are we so terrified lest God should speak to us? Because we know that if God does speak, either the thing must be done or we must tell God we will not obey Him."[2]

Notice that God manifested His presence through a fire and waited. The Lord didn't scream out at Moses as he passed. He waited until Moses did a re-take and began to approach the bush before He started communicating. Imagine how Moses' life would have been different if he had merely noticed the bush at a glance. What would have happened if he had shrugged off the bush as just another dried-up desert plant that had spontaneously combusted? Imagine how his destiny might have changed if he had never taken that first step toward the blazing bush. He may have gone about his normal duties for many more years, never really discovering God's divine purpose for his life. He would have missed out on the parting of the Red Sea, the manna, and all the other miracles the Lord performed in freeing the Jews from bondage. But Moses didn't brush off the burning bush. He took the time to take a closer look.

Likewise, when we stop brushing off the story of salvation as just a tradition and take the time to step aside and look more closely at the great I Am, He will speak to us just as He did to Moses.

And so He began to speak to me—a young woman who cut my teeth on church pews and knew the Bible cover to cover. Like Moses, raised by a devout mother, I had learned the fundamentals of the faith. But knowing the fundamentals of the faith is not the same as stepping aside to gaze upon the fiery presence of a God so holy and so complete that He doesn't need physical fuel. Only when I paused to gaze did I begin a radical journey to discerning His voice, discovering His perfect will, and moving heaven with my prayers. According to J. I. Packer,

> Meditation is a lost art today, and Christian people suffer grievously from their ignorance of the practice. Meditation is the activity of calling to mind, thinking over, and dwelling on and applying to oneself, the various things that one knows about the works and ways and purposes and promises of God. It is an activity of holy

thought, consciously performed in the presence of God, under the eye of God, by the help of God, as a means of communion with God.[3]

Removing the Sandals

One of the first things that God told Moses to do was take off his sandals, because the place he stood was holy. The bush and surrounding terrain weren't holy within themselves. The presence of God was holy, and everything His presence touched radiated with His holiness.

God's asking Moses to remove his sandals holds multiple meanings. First, it was considered an act of respect in their culture to remove the shoes, as removing the hat to go indoors is today. So on a very basic level, God was telling Moses to show respect. However, once Moses took off his sandals, he wasn't going anywhere until he put them back on. The desert is no place for a barefoot stroll. Aside from the issue of respect, I believe God was also indicating that Moses was going to be there awhile. And so he was; the conversation with God spans nearly two chapters of the Bible and deals with a variety of issues.

So it is with us. When we turn aside to gaze upon the Lord, we must be willing to "take off our shoes" and commit time to listen to Him. Otherwise, we will hear only part of what God has to say to us and understand only a fraction of all He wants to show and teach us.

William W. Walford said it like this:

Sweet hour of prayer, sweet hour of prayer,

That calls me from a world of care

And bids me at my Father's throne

Make all my wants and wishes known!

In seasons of distress and grief

My soul has often found relief,

And oft escaped the tempter's snare,

By thy return, sweet hour of prayer.

Sweet hour of prayer, sweet hour of prayer,

The joy I feel, the bliss I share,

Of those whose anxious spirits burn

With strong desires for thy return!

With such I hasten to the place

Where God, my Saviour, shows His face,

And gladly take my station there,

And wait for thee, sweet hour of prayer.

Sweet hour of prayer, sweet hour of prayer,

Thy wings shall my petition bear

To Him whose truth and faithfulness

Engage the waiting soul to bless;

And since He bids me seek His face,

Believe His word, and trust His grace,

I'll cast on Him my ev–'ry care,

And wait for thee, sweet hour of prayer.[4]

On another level, removing the sandals can be symbolic of God's asking us to take off or set aside anything that might come between us and Him . . . anything that would ultimately stop us from touching holy ground. This can come in the form of sin, coping mechanisms, attitudes, emotional or spiritual wounds, or bondage to the past. Sometimes these "sandals" are layered in our hearts. God asks us to take them off one at a time.

And so it was with me. God in His mercy asked me to relinquish my own "sandals" one layer at a time. He then began a process of healing and deliverance. With each layer I released, I was able to sense His presence all the more. And even today I am continually amazed at the new areas of freedom where He leads me.

However, my willingness to relinquish these "sandals" to God one at a time was superseded by a decision to release my will—the very essence of who I was—to the control and guidance of a holy creator. That point of surrender within our hearts is what drives our desire for a holy romance.

First Things First

According to C. S. Lewis, "You can't get second things by putting them first; you can get second things only by putting first things first."[6] Stormie Omartian states, "Your relationship with the Lord must always have top priority over everything else. The Lord said, 'You shall have no other gods

The beginning of power is

consciously opening our minds to

God and being receptive to

His presence, His Spirit,

His voice and His will.

—Charles L. Allen[5]

before Me' (Exodus 20:3), and He means it. God wants your undivided attention. When you seek Him first every day and ask Him to help you put your life in order, He will do that."[7] You may be thinking that you're so ready for God to put your life in order and you're eager to remove your own "sandals," but that initial desire will breed a conflict within your inner self if you have not fully surrendered that self to the lordship of Christ. According to David A. Seamands, "Self-surrender is the ultimate crisis because it is the all-inclusive crisis, encompassing all other crises of life. . . . Self-surrender is both a definite crisis and a never-ending process. When we talk about self-surrender we are talking about a commitment of your will to the lordship of Christ."[8] Until we make this commitment, there is a struggle within our hearts over whether or not we will wholly commit our lives to the divine romance, and we often find ourselves caught in patterns of sin that seem to have control over us. The apostle Paul put it like this:

> We know that the law is spiritual; but I am unspiritual, sold as a slave to sin. I do not understand what I do. For what I want to do I do not do, but what I hate I do. And if I do what I do not want to do, I agree that the law is good. As it is, it is no longer I myself who do it, but it is sin living in me. I know that nothing good lives in me, that is, in my sinful nature. For I have the desire to do what is good, but I cannot carry it out. For what I do is

not the good I want to do; no, the evil I do not want to do—this I keep on doing *(Romans 7:14-19)*.

When the Lord told Moses to remove his sandals, there was no argument or struggle. He removed them without hesitation. Likewise, only when we place our will in the hands of the Lord are we willing to say as did Samuel, "Speak, for your servant is listening" (1 Samuel 3:10).

When I began my own journey, I came to such a crisis experience early in my teen years. However, I believe many times God asks us to renew that commitment as our knowledge of Him grows and we reach new levels of maturity. Different denominations have different names and descriptions for this experience. Some call it "making Him Lord of your life." Some call it "baptism in the Holy Spirit." Others refer to it as "the fullness of the Spirit." Those like Oswald Chambers label it "sanctification."

According to Chambers,

"And the very God of peace sanctify you wholly" (1 Thessalonians 5:23, KJV). When we pray to be sanctified, are we prepared to face the standard of these verses? We take the term sanctification much too lightly. Are we prepared for what sanctification will cost? It will cost an intense narrowing of all our interests on earth, and an immense broadening of all our interests in God. Sanctification means intense concentration on God's point of view. . . . Are we prepared for God to do in us all that

He separated us for? . . . The reason some of us have not entered into the experience of sanctification is that we have not realized the meaning of sanctification from God's standpoint. Sanctification means being made one with Jesus so that the disposition that ruled Him will rule us. Are we prepared for what that will cost? It will cost everything that is not of God in us.[9]

And so it is that when we tell God we want more of Him, He in turn asks for all of us. So many people get to this point and balk. Thoughts of a divine romance hold such promise of reward that many are enticed to the process. But for every step we take toward God, He will ask us to remove or release yet another thing in our mind, heart, or spirit that hinders us from being progressively more like Him. Unfortunately, many want the reward of the holy romance without the sacrifice of self. According to Stormie Omartian, "Holiness means being sanctified by Jesus. Once we have received Jesus, we can't continue to live our old sinful lifestyle. Now that we have Him living in us and the Holy Spirit guiding us and transforming us, we have no excuse."[10]

Corrie ten Boom tells the story of a lady planning a meeting in a room in her house. She reported to her brother that the room was filled with women during the first meeting. The next week, she told him the room was fuller. The third week, she reported that the room was even fuller. Skeptical, the brother told her that was impossible. She replied that it was

Prayer is an offering up

of our desires unto God

for things agreeable

to His will.

—Westminster Shorter Catechism

certainly possible, because with each week that progressed, she removed pieces of furniture to make room for more ladies. Ten Boom goes on to say, "You can be filled with the Holy Spirit, and be still more filled. Perhaps some furniture must be moved out of your heart . . . 'that Christ will be more and more at home in your hearts'" (Ephesians 3:17, TLB).

As we develop the divine romance, He is guaranteed to ask us to release "furniture" so that He may fill us completely. Whatever He asks of you, do it. Dare to follow in Moses' footsteps and turn aside to listen. When you hear, don't hesitate to rush to the task of obedience. Your spiritual power and effectiveness hinges on your willingness to remove your "furniture," your "sandals"—and yourself.

2
The Relationship

༄

He has showed you, O man, what
is good. And what does the LORD
require of you? To act justly and to
love mercy and to walk humbly
with your God *(Micah 6:8)*.

My son, Brett, and I have much in common. Among other things, we have identical personality types and share the same sense of humor. We spend a lot of time laughing at things many people don't understand. Sometimes, Brett and I are falling out of our chairs in hysterics while my daughter and husband stare at us with you're-really-weird-for-thinking-that's-funny expressions on their faces.

We're so totally on the same wavelength there have been times we've broken into rhythmic banter, such as the recent round that mimicked the famous Dr. Seuss book, *Green Eggs and Ham*. It all revolved around Brett's wearing one of his fish shirts. He has several shirts that have fish on them. He enjoys fishing, so he buys dress shirts and T-shirts that reflect that love. Before our verbal exchange was over, we were spontaneously going back and forth in a round that ended with Brett saying, "I will not, will not in the dark, I would not, could not in the park. . . . I will not wear my fish shirt, I will not wear it, Mom-you-are." By this point, we were laughing out loud and feeling very smug and clever about ourselves. It was a moment we will remember for life.

What's amazing is that Brett is fourteen. Many four-teen-year-old boys have no desire to hang out with or talk to their moms. Most can give you at least fifty reasons why that would *not* be a good idea! Some are more interested in what they can get away with than anything else. Even though Brett isn't perfect and he's had his moments, overall, we have a fabulous relationship. I'm very thankful that God has blessed me with such a phenomenal son who actually enjoys being with good old mom.

But then, I have taken the time to purposefully foster this relationship from the time he was born. I've spent hours listening to him, I show him that I value his opinion, and I've invested time in doing the things he wants to do. When he was five, I slid down the McDonald's tunnel slide until I felt as if I had spent an hour in the spin cycle of a washing machine. When he was ten, it meant riding bikes all over the neighborhood. Now that he's fourteen, it means we go fishing and swimming. We also play video games. I am now reaping the benefits of all that invested energy. But when you think about it, a phenomenal relationship with *anyone* comes only when we purposefully invest energies into growing and improving that relationship.

As a result, I'm in tune with Brett's feelings and thoughts. I've taken the time to get to know him well enough that I know by his tone of voice, what he's feeling, and often, what he's thinking. No matter how well one of his friends might try to mimic his voice, I would be able to tell he or she was faking it. I know Brett's voice that well.

But what if I had never known Brett? What if we were separated by adoption when he was born, perhaps, and I didn't get to watch him grow up? I wouldn't immediately recognize his voice if he called by phone. As a matter of fact,

I might even be fooled into believing an imposter was Brett, especially if he arrived with documentation and a story that matched my own. From there I could develop a pseudo-relationship with "my son," and live the rest of my life believing the lie that an imposter was Brett.

Tragically, this is what people can do with God as well. They don't take the time to seriously invest in a relationship with the Lord and are eventually convinced a religious lifestyle is intimacy with God. Or they never really encounter Jesus in the first place. They grow up in a church and learn the language. They believe they have a relationship when they merely have a learned way of behavior.

As a result, they develop a pseudo-relationship with "God." They think they hear His voice. In reality, they are hearing a "recording" in their brains that has been placed there through religious training steeped in legalism, tradition, or prejudices. And just as the Jewish leaders thought they were doing God a favor by crucifying Jesus, these people are convinced they are embracing an intimate relationship with God by adhering to the falsehoods programmed into their minds. In reality, they have been fooled into accepting a misrepresentation of the real thing.

Legalism

When people replace intimacy with God with legalism, it can take one of two forms: applauding themselves for obeying rules; or feeling good about themselves because they don't obey strict rules. Those who rigidly obey rules are usually very good at listing off all the main things that God expects. Often these are the things they have been taught that God expects and are not representative of true moral issues. They have all these rules memorized, strictly follow them, and are ready to impose their list upon anyone. They base their experience with God on how well they can follow church policies. The closer they adhere to the rules, the more they "feel" God's approval. But it's really not God's approval they are feeling. It's the approval of the persons or religious groups who programmed their minds to interpret intimacy with God as a rule-based experience.

On the other hand, legalism can also take the form of those who think they are spiritually superior because they *don't* follow a long list of rigid rules. In such cases, they still measure their relationship with God by the rules. Since they are free from having to be so rule-conscious, they think they're a little more spiritual than their brothers and sisters who are all caught up in the rules. Their brand of legalism just happens to be based on the rules they *don't* follow rather than the ones they do; but it's still based on a relationship with the rules.

In reality, intimacy with God is not based on the rules or applauding yourself for following them or not. True intimacy with the Lord is founded upon the *time* we spend with

Him and our willingness to allow Him to carve us into His image. The more time we spend with Him, the greater the intimacy. According to Michael Phillips, "Spiritual development cannot be rushed. God is never in a hurry."[1] Obeying *His* commandments, not extraneous man-made rules, will grow out of this spiritual development. But the believer recognizes the source of the strength to obey, and it certainly isn't by his or her own power.

To stop me from personally falling into either trap, I have memorized Micah 6:8. It is my theme verse for life: "He has showed you, O man, what is good. And what does the LORD require of you? To act justly and to love mercy and to walk humbly with your God." If I can fulfill just these three requirements, I have gone a long way to pleasing God and furthering my relationship with Him. Focusing on Micah 6:8 also keeps me tuned in to the big picture of what God expects. It stops me from getting hung up on the dozens of little things that can become a legalistic stumbling block.

Tradition

For generations, people have confused the voice of God and a relationship with God with the voice of tradition. People misconstrue "the way we've always done things" with God's perfect will. From there they assume that if anyone doesn't do things "the way they've always been done," then that person must not have a relationship with God. Many people have been programmed to believe all sorts of things that actually put God into a cultural box—*our* culture in *our* time—and freeze Him in the image of *our* religious trappings. Once God has been recreated in the image of our culture and our traditions, people erroneously assume that the more stringently they adhere to tradition, the more they are in line with the mind of Christ. Unfortunately, some of these traditions can even violate the heart of Christ, His love, and the freedom He came to offer all those who believe in Him.

Religious leaders were doing exactly this when Jesus Christ was on earth. Not only did He hammer at their legalism and their hypocrisy, but He also attacked their adherence to tradition over mercy. In Mark 7:9-13 Jesus said,

> You have a fine way of setting aside the commands of God in order to observe your own traditions! For Moses said, "Honor your father and your mother," and, "Anyone who curses his father or mother must be put to death." But you say that if a man says to his father or mother: "Whatever help you might otherwise have received from me is Corban" (that is, a gift devoted to God), then you no longer let him do anything for his father or mother. Thus you nullify the word of God by your tradition that you have handed down. And you do many things like that.

Essentially, Christ was referencing a tradition that allowed people to use a loophole to get out of giving assistance to their parents. If a person designated money as a gift unto God, then he didn't have to give his parents that money—even though he might not release the money to the church for years. In other words, in a society without social security and other programs that helped the elderly, an individual was allowed to rob his parents of sustenance under the traditional guise of keeping money for the church. In short, they clung to tradition over mercy as a means to furthering their own pocketbooks.

So many times, that is what happens when people place tradition as God in their lives. The traditions must be obeyed no matter what, because they hold a God-like place in the hearts of those who worship them. And people clinging to those traditions are willing to verbally slit throats in order to defend their "God."

There are many areas in churches where people confuse God's voice with tradition. Furthermore, I've witnessed people going at each other to defend all sorts of traditions. One issue that serves as a good example from the recent past has involved styles of church music. Churches have split because some people believe God approves of only one style of music. Ironically, those who rabidly defend tradition—and those who don't—both believe they are hearing the voice of God and strengthening their relationship with him by adhering to their method of worship.

The truth is that each generation usually redefines what its experience with God is going to sound like musically. When the younger groups come on the scene with new sounds, they are actually creating a tradition. If they are not careful, they will be the ones in years to come rabidly defending their tradition as God's only approved mode of worship.

For instance, when many of the old, traditional hymns were written by John and Charles Wesley, they were set to contemporary bar tunes. The traditionalists of their time rejected these songs as too contemporary and worldly. These traditionalists thought they were "hearing the voice of God" in rejecting the music. No way would God approve of such! Now these same hymns are embraced as the traditional cornerstone of the worship experience for many. Ironically, those who are bound by tradition are now "hearing the voice of God" telling them that those old songs—and *only* those songs—should be sung. Meanwhile, many of the younger crowd are embracing the contemporary praise music and believe that God is directing them to break away from the old hymns.

Both groups firmly believe they are hearing God's voice— just as strongly as the traditionalists who originally rejected the hymns believed they were hearing God's voice. Ironically, they can't both be hearing the voice of God, telling them to do opposite things in the same church. This is a clear example of getting the voice of God confused with a "recording" in the brain that has been placed there by people's influence, not by God's design. Could it be that both groups are simply defin-

31

ing their worship experience by what moves them and then expecting everyone to bend to their needs?

In the church my husband and I pastor, we try to blend contemporary choruses with the traditional hymns. We even read the stories behind many of the hymns so the younger generation can tap into the deeper meaning. We believe God has spoken and still speaks through many styles of music—both past and present. It's up to us to be open to what He has shown all generations, not just ours.

This way, we hold God's viewpoint, rather than trying to conform Him to *our* culture and *our* tastes. But the ability to have God's viewpoint means we have to go so deep with Him that we stop making our traditions our God and start seeking *Him* as God. We must be willing to allow Him to reprogram our minds to conform to His thoughts on every tradition. Styles of music is but one example where this is a must. Many other areas prevail.

I challenge you to lay your traditions at the feet of Jesus and ask Him to examine your heart to make certain you aren't clinging to traditions as a substitute for tuning into His voice. Be courageous enough to view traditions for what they often are—simply a way we've gotten used to doing things. Understand that many times there's nothing wrong with traditions. It's how we view them and what place they hold in our hearts and minds that makes them wrong. When we start viewing our own traditions as the way God always expects us to do things, we are in jeopardy of making our traditions our God. Furthermore, when our passion for our traditions is stronger than our passion for God, we must ask Him to put them into balance in our lives.

According to Oswald Chambers,

> If the Spirit of God detects anything in you that is wrong, He does not ask you to put it right; He asks you to accept the light, and He will put it right. A child of the light confesses instantly and stands bared before God; a child of the darkness says—"Oh, I can explain that away." When once the light breaks and the conviction of wrong comes, be a child of the light, and confess, and God will deal with what is wrong; if you vindicate yourself, you prove yourself to be a child of the darkness.[2]

Prejudices

When we hear the word "prejudices," most people in the United States think of racial prejudices. However, prejudices can take the forms of economic, gender, and denominational, as well as racial. In the United States slave era many Christians used the Word of God to prove that owning slaves was God's perfect will for them. They believed they were hearing the voice of God confirming their assumptions. Some Christians can't stand rich people and believe with all their hearts that no wealthy person can really be holy. Likewise, others believe that if someone is in poverty, he or she must not possess God's blessings or experience His presence. Still others twist the Word of God to prove gender prejudices. I have heard sermons and read books that were dedicated to proving that one gender is superior to the other in God's eyes. Some even insist that God regards the prayers and decisions of one over the other.

Christians who interpret Scripture in a prejudicial manner and embrace prejudices as a substitute for the voice of God have fallen prey to the ultimate deception. What they are really hearing is the voice of their own carnal needs to elevate themselves, rather than God's voice. If they ever took the time to be still before God and simply read the words of Jesus when He said, "So in everything, do to others what you would have them do to you, for this sums up the Law and the Prophets" (Matthew 7:12), they would find that they would be called to release prejudices or be in disobedience to the Lord.

In Galatians 3:28 Paul summed up what should be our attitude: "There is neither Jew nor Greek, slave nor free, male nor female, for you are all one in Christ Jesus." This one scripture covers the prejudices of race (Jew/Greek), financial status (slave/free), and gender (male/female). In Christ we all are one, and when Christians truly are in a relationship with Christ, unity prevails.

There is one other prejudice that erects its head too often in Christian circles. My husband and I have traveled all over the United States and have spoken and sung in so many different denominations that we have lost count. I'm continually astounded at the number in every denomination who believe that God likes their group better. I call this denominational prejudice. They haven't taken the time to sit with the Lord long enough to allow Him to show them that He loves each and every worker in His kingdom, regardless of the label on the church door. Each denomination has its purpose, and He works within each one. We have felt the presence of God in most churches where we have ministered, no matter the denominational label. We have been open to His voice, and He has spoken to us and empowered us. As the body of believers, we must be willing to set aside our differences and bind together in unity on what we agree upon.

Unfortunately, people can place their denomination as God in their lives just as easily as they can legalism, prejudices, or their traditions. They become a Methodist, Episcopalian, Baptist, Pentecostal, or Nazarene first and a Christian second. In their minds, they carve God in the image of their denomination. The more they work for their denomination, the greater they believe their intimacy with God to be. Oswald Chambers states, "Beware of any work for God which enables you to evade concentration on Him. A great many Christian workers worship their work."[3] It's not a matter of "Can this happen?" It's a matter of "This will happen" when God's people don't pursue pure intimacy with Him first and service and allegiance to their denomination as an overflow of a divine romance.

The Real Thing

Even though some people do fall into a pseudo-relationship with Christ, many strive to get in touch with God's presence as more than a mere concept or theory. Many desire to know that God is deep inside them and try to become aware of His presence in their hearts. True seekers want God's touch inwardly and outwardly. It's not enough to know about God intellectually. Likewise, it's not enough to settle for a pseudo-relationship with Him. True seekers want a relationship that is the real thing. They want to encounter God as the One who saves and liberates from meaningless life. They want to know him as the God whose presence burns at the deepest level of their beings.

According to Sandra D. Wilson,

Genuine relational intimacy doesn't develop quickly. Or accidentally. We need to cultivate an environment in which intimacy can flourish. And we do this by practicing habits like listening to and giving undivided attention to the person with whom we want to be close. As we practice such habits over time, we really get to know someone. Relational intimacy grows.[5]

The Bible tells us that at a certain time and place in history, God himself was fully embodied and revealed as Jesus of Nazareth. For this reason, Jesus is called Messiah, King of Kings, Lord of Lords, and Savior. Also, the gospels tell

Learning to walk with God is a

process. And just when we think

we have it all figured out, God

leads us to a new place where our

old tricks won't work. In fact,

it may seem like we're learning

how to walk all over again.

And in a way we are.

We enter unfamiliar territory

and are soon reminded that,

on our own, we stumble.

—Stormie Omartian[4]

us that this same Jesus Christ, God's only Son, is also in us as our Savior. And it is through Him that we have intimacy with God the Father. If we seek Him with all that we are, the Spirit through which God created all things is alive in the very center of our hearts. He is within all who are willing to set aside all they are and all they think for all He is. In Romans 5:2 Paul writes, "And we rejoice in the hope of the glory of God." This is the glory of wholeness of the present life, and the glory of the life to come.

Jesus said in John 14:23, "If anyone loves me, he will obey my teaching. My Father will love him, and we will come to him and make our home with him." In John 17:20-23 He said, "I pray also for those who will believe in me through their [apostles] message, that all of them may be one, Father, just as you are in me and I am in you. May they also be in us so that the world may believe that you have sent me. I have given them the glory that you gave me, that they may be one as we are one: I in them and you in me."

So many Christians seem to find little cause for rejoicing. Unfortunately, many are sitting on church pews believing they are tuned in to God when they really are not. The search for happiness apart from intimacy with God eventually leads to dead-end frustration. When people are "trying God" as they try on a pair of gloves, rather than allowing God to immerse them in His presence, they get nowhere.

Jesus told us that accepting God's love and entering into a lifelong love affair with Him is what life is all about.

Only by allowing God to sweep away all our learned religious trappings—our prejudices, our legalism—and accepting God's intense love do we become whole. Out of this wholeness comes the strength to love other people in a life-changing way. We can do this with our lives—but only if they are founded on the solid rock of a loving relationship with God. God took the initiative when He gave himself to us. And when we begin to rejoice in the discovery of what God feels like deep within us, we simultaneously begin to discover how to rejoice in our relationships with others.

This is the cornerstone for my relationship with my son. I have allowed God to love him through me. Every human relationship is turned to gold when this level of love is achieved.

If we try to build relationships apart from intimacy with God, we end up hurting rather than healing one another. When I counsel engaged couples, I tell them that when you spend a couple of years courting one another, you get to know the person. Then during the first two years of marriage, you get acquainted with that person's issues. Whether in a marriage, friendship, or extended family relationships, everyone has issues that he or she will never be delivered from without a genuine relationship with Christ. Jesus sent out His disciples to represent God's kingdom, to reflect His

There is hunger in our hearts that is never satisfied, except by Jesus. Do you feel lonesome and hungry? Do you have problems that you can't solve? Do you feel chased, with no way out?

Come to Him.

—Corrie ten Boom[6]

love, and to heal others. They were to have the kind of relationship He had with the Father. That's what He wants us to do as well. When our relationship with Him is as powerful a force in our lives as it was in theirs, then and only then do we tap into the source of love that will empower us to bring about healing, rather than pain, in all our relationships.

The Example

Mark 1:35 states, "Very early in the morning, while it was still dark, Jesus got up, left the house and went off to a solitary place, where he prayed." As believers, we recognize that Jesus Christ was the sinless Son of God. We look to Him as our supreme example in all we do. If Jesus Christ needed time alone with the Father, to drink of that spiritual intimacy, how much more is it so with us?

If you're like me, you may feel that free moments are rare. All sorts of activities and responsibilities constantly pull at you: 40-plus hours of work, people to see, things to do, PTA, Boy Scouts, Girl Scouts, Sunday School lesson preparation, board meetings, gardening, miles to travel, school work, and the list never ends! Occasionally you may think you hardly have time to breathe, much less pray.

Jesus himself knew pressure-packed days. The day before He awoke early to pray, He had spent a full day healing people, teaching in the synagogue, and even casting out evil spirits. That Sabbath drained Him. I'm sure He dropped off to sleep as soon as He lay on his bed mat. But early the next morning before daylight, Jesus awoke, got up, slipped out of the house, and found a solitary place. There He prayed. After an exhausting day, He received the physical rest He needed. And now before the beginning of another hectic day, He would receive the strength and guidance He needed.

Interesting enough, the word "praying" here means far more than asking. It involves a moving toward God that is driven by a deep desire to worship and know Him. It embodies the true essence of worship. Understand that true prayer is entering into the presence of God and involves communion, fellowship, agreement, and a oneness with Him. As we enter into His presence with an attitude of submission that says He is Lord of our lives, we begin to be renewed. This renewal takes place as the purity and power of God begin to flow through us. As a dry sponge soaks up the water it's immersed in, so we soak up the presence and love of God.

In Matthew 6:7-8 Jesus said, "When you pray, do not keep babbling like pagans, for they think they will be heard because of their many words. Do not be like them, for your Father knows what you need before you ask him." After reading this passage, we might easily think, *If God is our Father, and a father supplies the needs of his children without them having to ask, then why pray?* Prayer is more than bringing a list of needs to God. Jesus told us that the Father knows our needs and that He is working to supply those needs. Even though it is important for us to state our needs to the Father, prayer provides communion with our Creator and Lord. Understand that entering into His presence is a far greater prayer than bringing Him a list of the things we need. Jesus knew this truth. If we follow His example, then so should we.

According to John Killinger,

> If there is one sin that hurts us more than all others, it is surely the sin of not praying. We are meant to live in the Spirit of the Lord—to live joyously, vibrantly, and lovingly in the world. But if we do not pray we cannot live in the Spirit. It is as simple as that. We lack the daily "connection" to God that would make such a wonderful life possible.[7]

Jesus, the sinless Son of God, recognized His need for that daily connection and thus demonstrated his own dependence upon the Father. That's why He got up before everyone else and went off by himself. Sometimes my own journey starts out in the wee hours of the morning, but not always. Some days my communion with God happens later in the day. The important thing is that intimate fellowship happens. Otherwise, we find ourselves substituting service to God for intimacy with God and allowing other forces and influences to blot out His voice. From there, we fall into a pseudo-relationship with Him and drift so far from Him that we forget what the real thing feels like and can no longer detect His voice.

Prayer is the gateway

to God's heart.

—Claire Cloninger[8]

3
The strength

❧

The LORD is my strength and my
shield; my heart trusts in him, and
I am helped. My heart leaps for joy
and I will give thanks to him
in song *(Psalm 28:7).*

The Valley of the Shadow of Death

My grandmother used to say that giving birth to a child was equated with going through the valley of the shadow of death. As a young teen, I didn't argue with her, even before I had my son. She gave birth to five children—two of them at once. I figure if anybody knew about the valley of the shadow of death, it would be her.

In my later teen years, I got a job as a nurse's aid and worked in the obstetrics ward quite a bit. That means that when I was the tender ages of sixteen to eighteen, I watched women give birth. I saw the pain, the agony, the distress. I saw it all! I also helped in the nursery with the newborns. I had an early education about the upheaval of childbirth and the high maintenance of babies.

Therefore, I decided rip-your-guts-out pain in the valley of the shadow of death was one thing I just didn't want to endure. For many years after my marriage, I knew I could do just fine without the excruciating experience of labor. But after ten and a half years, the baby bug hit Daniel and me, and we decided we should have a family. I tried really hard to suppress the memories of all those women in labor and just told myself to look ahead to the baby I would hold when the delivery was over.

Toward the end of my pregnancy, I developed pregnancy-induced hypertension. My high blood pressure was a sure ticket to my spending the month before the delivery in bed. The constant nausea that never went away was only worsened by feeling as if I had been hit over the head by a two-by-four because of the high blood pressure. On top of that, Brett was like a kicking kangaroo! By the time my day of induced labor arrived, I was so tired of being in bed, being nauseated, and sharing my body with a kicking machine, I was glad for the contraction pains to begin. However, we did not expect what happened once I was in the hard throes of labor.

First, my pain killer, an epidural, did not work. When I tried to tell the anesthesiologist, he patronized me. The nurse didn't seem to believe me any more than he did. By the time my labor pains felt like hot knives being driven through my abdomen, they believed me—especially since my blood pressure was up to stroke level. That's when the anesthesiologist came into the room and stood at the head of my bed while the nurse very quietly freaked out! She refused to look at my husband. When he asked her, "Is she going to be all right?" the nurse pretended not to hear. By this point, I was in the valley of the shadow of death. And the shadow was as dark as night. I had been pushing hard for nearly an hour, and Brett wasn't budging.

While my blood pressure continued to inch up (approximately 180+/120+) Daniel broke down and cried. He said all he could think was that he was going to have to raise the baby without a mother. The rising panic in the nurse's eyes only underscored his assumption.

But during the darkest moments of the labor, I had an invisible visitor. I will never forget that distinctive presence that arrived at my side and simply whispered to my soul, "It's all going to be all right." I began to cry as I experienced a divine touch that I cannot explain. The presence was not like the wonderful spirit that enters a room during a powerful church service when the Holy Spirit fills the place. No, this was the definite manifestation of a bodily form, but I could not see him. I could only feel him there as strongly as I would have been able to feel my husband standing at my side. I believe I had a visit either from my guardian angel or from the One the Old Testament refers to as the Angel of the Lord—Christ himself. Whatever the case, a blessed peace and strength swept through my spirit. I knew beyond doubt that I would not die—that the baby would be born soon.

That is exactly what happened. Before long, Daniel was saying, "He's here, Debra! Brett is here!" The raspy sound of a baby's first vocal eruption filled the room. The entire staff laughed with relief. My blood pressure eased back down, and I moved out of the valley of the shadow of death.

By the time I was holding Brett, I was madly in love. I knew all the pain was worth having our son. While many say mothers forget the pain of childbirth, I can't testify to that. Even fourteen and a half years later, I still vividly recall

Even though I walk through the

valley of the shadow of death,

I will fear no evil, for you are

with me; your rod and your staff,

they comfort me.

—Psalm 23:4

everything I told you and a lot of gory details I have withheld. Daniel was so shaken he said, "I can't go through that again!" I think watching me knock on the door of eternity was harder on him than it was on me. But then, I had my invisible visitor who gave me peace, courage, and strength.

Christ's Strength

Many who have walked with the Lord can testify to an amazing strength that has come upon them during a crisis or stayed with them just to help them survive their day-to-day life. Psalm 34:7-8 states, "The angel of the LORD encamps around those who fear him, and he delivers them. Taste and see that the LORD is good; blessed is the man who takes refuge in him." This amazing strength that the Angel of the Lord gives to us is beyond human understanding or ability.

As already mentioned, The Angel of the Lord is Jesus Christ, and His strength is too often underestimated by our limited knowledge. Many people erroneously depict Jesus Christ as a passive man with lily-white skin and a certain weakness that is covered with the label "meek." But the truth is, Jesus Christ was the strongest person who ever lived. True meekness is not weakness—it's harnessed strength. His love for sinners was as strong as His passion to confront the abusive religious leaders.

While numerous individuals faced crucifixion during the Roman era, none of them but Christ *chose* to be crucified. He had the power to summon leagues of angels to his rescue, but He chose the path of sacrifice for our sins. He possessed the unbelievable strength to face a tortuous, shameful death that makes me cringe when I even consider it. There's no childbirth experience even half as bad as what He went through.

When our congregation was leaving the movie theater after watching Mel Gibson's *The Passion of the Christ,* I recall a woman saying, "It really wasn't that bad." I nearly turned to her and said, "Actually, it was much worse than the movie depicted." While that movie did portray a brutal death, it omitted many gruesome details that would have probably left the whole audience nauseous—or worse.

When they beat Jesus with the cat-of-nine-tails, the whip was embedded with thorns and glass that dug into the skin while the whip slammed against the victim's back and wrapped around his abdomen. As the soldier pulled the whip back, chunks of flesh were ripped from the body. Many victims were actually disemboweled and died from the whipping alone.

By the time Jesus Christ was nailed to the cross, he was far from the smooth-skinned image we so often see in paintings. His flesh was torn and bleeding to the point of being grotesque. Some of his rib bones were very likely exposed due to missing flesh. Not only was blood pouring from His hands and feet, but His whole body was literally a bloody mass of mangled skin.

Jesus knew he faced all this when He prayed in the Garden of Gethsemane. That's the reason He was sweating drops of blood. The stress of what He was facing unnerved Him to the point of blood coming from His pores. Paul S. Taylor writes,

> Although this medical condition is relatively rare, according to Dr. Frederick Zugibe (Chief Medical Examiner of Rockland County, New York) it is well-known, and there have been many cases of it. The clinical term is *hematohidrosis*. Around the sweat glands, there are multiple blood vessels in a net-like form. Under the pressure of great stress the vessels constrict. Then as the anxiety passes, the blood vessels dilate to the point of rupture. The blood goes into the sweat glands. As the sweat glands are producing a lot of sweat, it pushes the blood to the surface—coming out as droplets of blood mixed with sweat.[1]

Not only did Jesus Christ have to face physical torment, but He also faced spiritual torment when He bore the sin of all humanity. Imagine the weight and guilt of every sin that has ever been committed or is ever going to be committed. Despite this enormous level of stress, He still had the strength to release His will to the Father's and complete the crucifixion.

The doorway to the strength Christ displayed in the Garden of Gethsemane is opened only through this same release, "not my will, but yours be done" (Luke 22:42). According to Catherine Marshall,

A demanding spirit, with self-will as its rudder, blocks prayer. I understood that the reason for this is that God absolutely refuses to violate our free will; that therefore, unless self-will is voluntarily given up, even God cannot move to answer prayer.

Jesus could have avoided the Cross. He did not have to go up to Jerusalem the last time. He could have compromised with the priests, bargained with Caiaphas. He could have capitalized on his following and appeased Judas by setting up the beginning of an earthly Kingdom. Pilate wanted to release Him, all but begged Him to say the right words that would let him do so. Even in the Garden on the night of the betrayal, He had plenty of time and opportunity to flee. Instead, Christ used His free will to turn the decision over to His Father.[2]

When Christ released His will unto the Father, Luke further states, "An angel from heaven appeared to him and strengthened him" (Luke 22:43). So it goes with us. Releasing the situation to God is our ticket to a supernatural strength that is born on the wings of angels. As long as we try to maintain control, we limit the depths of the divine

Recognizing our helplessness

"deals a mortal blow to the

most serious sin of all—man's

independence that ignores God."

—Catherine Marshall[5]

romance and harness the strength that is readily available to us through Christ's shed blood.

But too many times we insist on being dependent upon ourselves and strong within our own power. According to Stormie Omartian, "We try to make it on our own because we think that dependency is a sign of weakness, instead of understanding that it signals our willingness to allow God to be strong in us. If you are at a place in your life where you feel like you can't take one step without the Lord's help, be glad. He has you where He wants you."[3] Catherine Marshall further states, "This giving up of the self-will is the hardest thing we human beings are ever called on to do."[4]

Samson's Strength

While Christ reveals to us the perfect example of the releasing of our wills unto God's, Samson is the perfect example of one who did not relinquish his will to God's. Samson was self-reliant. (See Judges 13-16.) The Lord had given Samson a tremendous amount of physical strength as part of his Nazirite vow, which he was born into. He had more physical strength than any other biblical character, but he squandered this blessing through his lack of belief.

There are several flaws that contributed to Samson's downfall: his insistence on having whatever he wanted, his self-pride, and his desire to please. However, I believe his lack of belief in God's precepts tops his list of flaws. It would appear that Samson assumed that he could accept God's gifts without accepting God's call. In other words, he assumed he could bask in the blessings of holiness without living the holy life he had been set apart to live.

He may have gradually assumed that his strength was given for his own personal use. It seems never to have crossed his mind that his strength could be taken from him. Not until God left him (Judges 16:20) did Samson seem to realize that God had actually been with him in the first place. He was so self-reliant that he arrogantly assumed he was in control of his strength. His full belief in himself blinded him to his need for God. He had always been the master of his destiny, had always come out the victor, and had come to believe more in his own abilities than in God's.

As already mentioned, Samson was a Nazirite from birth. Because he was born into this special vow by God's ordination, he initially didn't choose to take the vow himself. His breaking the vow indicates that perhaps he never held it sacred in the first place. The three stipulations of the Nazirite vow were that he would not consume alcohol, he was not to touch a corpse, and he was not to cut his hair. Before Delilah ever arranged to cut his hair, Samson had already broken the Nazirite vows of drinking wine and handling dead bodies.

The famous story with Delilah lends itself to several interpretations. Many have assumed that Delilah tricked

Samson, but I believe that he full-well knew what she was up to. He thought *he* was toying with her.

Always "large and in charge," Samson assumes he forever will be. He first tells Delilah that he'll lose his strength if she binds him with seven fresh thongs. When that doesn't work, he claims that if he's tied with new ropes he'll lose his strength. Of course, that's false as well. He also lies that weaving the seven locks of his hair into a loom will make him a weakling. When that doesn't deplete his strength, he finally divulges the secret, ultimately enabling Delilah to arrange for the complete breaking of his Nazirite vow.

Scripture states that Delilah "put him to sleep on her lap," which indicates that perhaps she drugged him so that he was unaware when his hair was being cut (Judges 16:19). If this is true, then Samson probably thought that if they did try to cut his hair, he would wake up and catch them. But he didn't count on Delilah drugging him.

Sadly, many people play with God's graces as did Samson. They want the blessings and strength of the holy life without the sacrifice of obedience to God's commands—the ultimate relinquishment of self. Just like the entire nation of Israel, Samson had tremendous potential; but like the Israelites, he never understood that he had been called to be holy. Likewise, each individual has the potential for tremendous strength, but our belief in God as the ultimate source of our strength must be the bedrock for our spiritual existence.

Otherwise, we trifle with His call to "Be holy, because I am holy" (1 Peter 1:16), and we violate our own vow to Him.

According to Stormie Omartian, "Being holy is not being perfect. It's letting Him who is holy be in you. We can't be holy on our own, but we can make choices that allow holiness and purity to be manifested in our lives. We can separate ourselves from that which dilutes God's holiness in us. And we can do this because 'those who are Christ's have crucified the flesh with its passions and desires' (Galatians 5:24). We are able to live pure lives consecrated to the Lord."[6]

While some renege on their pursuit of holiness, others are born and raised in church, much as Samson was born into his Nazirite vow, and live a churchy routine without ever stepping into full commitment to Christ. Samson flirted with sin, and it cost him his strength. We are no different.

As already mentioned, Samson could have easily assumed that he would awaken if they actually tried to cut his hair, but there's the strong possibility that Delilah drugged him. So often this is where Satan gets us as well. He lulls us to sleep with the "spiritual drug" of complacency, and we drift so far from the voice of God that we aren't even aware we've lost His strength. Like those who dance on the edge of willful, known sin, perhaps when Samson broke the first Nazirite vows and apparently got away with it, he thought breaking the final vow wouldn't make any difference. Was this last vow the most important? Or did the consequences domino because it was the last vow he broke, and by doing so he stepped across a line that he had been balancing on for a long time?

With the cutting of his hair, Samson makes his disregard and rejection of his vow complete. He arrogantly assumes that he can break his vow and still keep his strength. According to Adam Clarke,

> The miraculous strength of Samson must not be supposed to reside either in his hair or in his muscles, but in that relation in which he stood to God as a Nazirite, such a person being bound by a solemn vow to walk in a strict conformity to the laws of his Maker. It was a part of the Nazirite's vow to permit no razor to pass on his head; and his long hair was the mark of his being a Nazirite, and of his vow to God. When Samson permitted his hair to be shorn off, he renounced and broke his Nazirite vow, in consequence of which God abandoned him.[7]

Tragedy heaps upon tragedy after Samson's choice. Judges 16:21 states, "Then the Philistines seized him, gouged out his eyes and took him down to Gaza. Binding him with bronze shackles, they set him to grinding in the prison." Sadly, Samson's loss of spiritual sight is followed by the loss of his physical sight. His physical imprisonment comes only after his spiritual bondage to self-reliance.

The story ends with Samson's hair growing back and scripture thus implies that his strength returned. Adam

Clarke states, "And may we not suppose that, sensible of his sin and folly, he renewed his Nazirite vow to the Lord, in consequence of which his supernatural strength was again restored?"[8] His returned strength enables him to push down the columns in a pagan temple. In the end he kills a host of Philistine rulers, along with himself.

In some ways, Samson is a symbolic forerunner of Christ. In chapter 13 we have already seen that Samson's birth was remarkably similar to the birth of Jesus. In chapter 16 we see similarities in their deaths: both were captured and mocked, both destroyed an enemy in their death, and both deaths brought salvation to many. The story of Samson points us forward to the much greater salvation of Jesus Christ.

However, Samson ceases to be like Christ after these points. While Jesus was completely free of sin and completely submitted to the Father, Samson was self-reliant and sinful. As He was dying Jesus prayed, "Father, forgive them, for they do not know what they are doing" (Luke 23:34). Samson's prayer before death, while finally recognizing God as his strength, was filled with revenge (Judges 16:28). While Jesus fully understood the reason He was on earth, Samson seemed to lack direction and an awareness of His strength having a God-ordained purpose.

According to Stormie Omartian,

> Each one of us has a purpose in the Lord. But many of us don't realize that. And when we don't have an accurate

understanding of our identity, we either strive to be like someone else or something we're not. We compare ourselves to others and feel as though we always fall short.

God doesn't want that for you. He wants you to have a clear vision for your life. He wants to reveal to you what your gifts and talents are and show you how to best develop them and use them for His glory.[9]

Our Strength

I believe that God desires to successfully replay the Samson story in our own lives when we are willing to allow Him to be strong in us. His unbelievable strength is available to us as long as we don't repeat Samson's mistake of becoming self-reliant. We are all warriors in the battle against evil and the struggle to survive whatever life throws at us—from difficult childbirth to the paralysis of a loved one. And Christ's desire for us is to exhibit the strength Samson initially exhibited on a spiritual level.

The Burnett family can testify to such a strength rising up within them when their son, Andy, was shot down in Iraq in 2008. During the heat of battle, a bullet that was fierce enough to slice through a brick wall entered the back of Andy's neck and forever changed his world. While some of his friends were killed in the attack, Andy survived. However, he was paralyzed from the neck down. The pain and dismay that Andy faced were felt just as strongly by his parents, Larry and Donna Burnett.

The son that I struggled to deliver is now fourteen. As the mother of a young teen, I find it hard to imagine that my son could join the armed forces in just four short years or that he would face enemy fire like other young heroes. The chilling thought of him going off to war is intensified by thoughts of him being paralyzed or killed. So many brave parents have received "the call" and grieved the loss or stood by their sons and daughters whose bodies are mangled.

The Burnetts are one such family. As members of a church on our denominational district, many of us have read their e-mails and kept up with Andy's progress while praying for their strength and a miracle for Andy's recovery. During the whole crisis the Burnetts have exemplified a strength that is beyond human capabilities.

In a letter about that strength, Larry Burnett writes,

Also, there is one detail that I wanted to clear up tonight while I have the opportunity, and I take the greatest joy in doing so. So many have written to encourage us and have been very complimentary to the strength of our faith. But actually, I felt compelled to be clear: it is not my faith that is strong—it is the faith of Christ in me.

The faith of this day actually was given to me as a gift on a summer afternoon more than 30 years ago. On that day, which came at the end of a long and humiliating personal struggle, God did something. It was on that afternoon that I was given access to the vitality of the living Christ as my personal resource from that day on.

On that afternoon I was praying for deliverance for what I had come to understand to be a pattern of personal failures since my conversion a few months before. I was asking God to help me, not really understanding in those days that there was even such a thing as a Spiritual baptism. But ignorant or not, I experienced it that day. God came in such an unmistakable way. I was certainly no theologian in those days, but I knew when I rose from my knees that I was somehow profoundly different.

Life itself changed for me right there. I have since come to understand through my experience and studies that I was immersed in the Spirit of the living Christ right there. I have also come to understand from the New Testament that as a result of that event so long ago now, as Paul said in Galatians 2:20, "The life I live in the body, I live by faith in the Son of God." Literally I was baptized into His faith back there. And it is this faith that has been growing up inside me ever since.

I know now, in these more mature years, that my faith would never have been sufficient for all that God has called me to over the years. My faith was only barely sufficient to get me to that Pentecostal merger where Jesus took over. Thank God for the Resurrection and the living Christ who is willing to become the sufficiency of His people in this most intimate way.

As a pastor, I see many trying to make their encounter with Christ to be just one more ordinary thing in their life that they can manage in ordinary ways. But this encounter is no ordinary thing. It is a life-changing phenomenon that is without equal. To know the empowerment of Christ within changes life itself. The approach to life is different, and the outcome is different. You just cannot make ordinary out of that. You cannot compartmentalize it to Sunday. And it cannot be consigned to the ordinary.

Since that first afternoon when I came to know God so intimately for the first time, I have become addicted to that intimacy. Every morning I seek to be refilled with His Spirit, and He grants that. I am allowed to live every day of my life in His energies and vitality. This is the unique and precious privilege of every New Testament Christian who has discovered life on the backside of a personal Pentecost; and that is anything but ordinary.

Out of that life force of the living Christ within grows our newness. Literally we are transformed by His influence over our character, our mind, our heart. Under the influence of His empowering Spirit, as He uses the dramas of this physical life, we grow out of the oversimplifications of our spiritual childhood and learn to be spiritually articulate. And all the while we grow closer to Him and discover Him and ourselves at new levels.

So I want to be clear. Larry is nowhere near equal to the challenges of this life. But I have simply discovered a resource that is way beyond Larry. It is the living Jesus. I love the Jesus of the Cross, but it is the Jesus of the resurrection that I know the best. We live together every day. And the honor and blessing is entirely mine.[10]

Clearly, Larry Burnett has tapped into a strength that is beyond his human capabilities—or mine. But he would not have had access to that strength had it not been for his willingness to relinquish all he had to God in exchange for all Christ had for him. This great exchange marks the beginning of a miraculous journey in which Christ's strength steers us through life, propelling us forward in victory or holding us up during defeat or grief.

However, when we don't pursue the divine romance, when we don't regularly fall silent for the great exchange—our nothingness for God's everything—like Samson we lose the focus of our purpose and our ability to "live and move and have our being" in Him (Acts 17:28). I would love to tell you that my journey to continually fall silent before Him is perfected, but I cannot. While my heart's cry is to sit for hours a day in His presence, there are some days that I wake up running and don't stop until I flop into bed. Although I start each day with my "Hour of Power in the Shower," as

The LORD is my strength and my

shield; my heart trusts in him,

and I am helped. My heart leaps

for joy and I will give thanks

to him in song. The LORD is the

strength of his people, a fortress of

salvation for his anointed one.

—Psalm 28:7-8

mentioned in chapter 4, that is no replacement for falling silent and absorbing God's presence—and His strength.

Even though I am an imperfect human being, I serve a perfect God. And God's grace is always available to meet me, even when I fall short. I have learned that He is as eager—or even more eager—to share the divine romance with me and impart His strength as I sit and absorb His presence. After all, that is why He created us—for a relationship. With Larry Burnett I can claim that I have become addicted to the holy intimacy that develops in the presence of a holy God. And I have learned that it is of monumental importance that I stay immersed in the holy of holies. Otherwise, I become as powerless as Samson and live nowhere near the miraculous strength that Christ exemplified.

4

The Power

∽✍∾

Finally, be strong in the Lord and
in his mighty power. Put on the
full armor of God so that you can
take your stand against the devil's
schemes. For our struggle is not
against flesh and blood, but against
the rulers, against the authorities,
against the powers of this dark
world and against the spiritual
forces of evil in the heavenly realms
(Ephesians 6:10-12).

⤳ I have five cats that I am certain will all live forever, considering the great care we give them. Of course, like most felines, they own our home and totally rule it. We are merely their guests whom they "graciously" allow to live there as long as we serve them appropriately.

One cat is particularly dominant. His name is Lucky. I rescued Lucky from the middle of the road about five years ago. Cars were zipping up and down the street, and he was cowering in the middle of traffic. I estimate that he was only about three weeks old, and his life was going to come to a quick end if somebody didn't save him. I decided that person had to be me.

Now that orange striped kitten has grown into an adult feline. My husband jokes that this cat has been declawed and neutered, and we still call him Lucky! Some days, I think we should change his name to Hitler. Many times he's the most affectionate cat you could ever want. But if he's having a Hitler moment and you happen to be walking by his "royal self" and he's not in the mood to see your face, he will look you square in the eyes, deliberately show his "fangs," and hiss at you. If you dare touch his superior fur, he will proceed to nip at you. There are some days that cat just needs to pray through!

Now we also have a cat named Tiger. Tiger is my prettiest kitty and my sweetest kitty. He's a gorgeous dark brown tabby. His stripes are nearly perfect. I've never known him to become aggressive toward a soul. His main goal is to love and be loved. His favorite hobbies are being rubbed and purring. Presently Tiger is about a fourth bigger than Lucky. He's stocky and muscular, while Lucky is lean like a panther.

However, when Lucky was about nine months old, Tiger was already full grown and was half again as big as Lucky. At that time, Lucky had already been de-clawed, and Tiger still had his claws. He also had the advantage of being a full-grown, male cat who had been around the yard defending himself for about five years.

I remember one morning looking out the back window and seeing Tiger on the patio and Lucky on the bottom step. Lucky had his de-clawed paw in the air, holding it over Tiger's head. And Tiger was cowering with his ears lowered in fear. His body language said, "Oh, Mr. Lucky, please, sir, kind sir, don't attack me, sir, kind sir." Ironically, Tiger was not only bigger than Lucky but also had front claws as well. If he had had the heart to, Tiger could have sprung up, given Lucky a roll or two, slashed his nose with sharp claws, and won a backyard fight that would have ensured Lucky's respect for years to come. But Tiger didn't do that. He cowered. The reason he cowered was because Lucky had Tiger bluffed into believing he was bigger and stronger. Lucky convinced Tiger that his harmless, raised paw was loaded with needle-like claws. To this day, Tiger is still a defeated foe in the face of Lucky's snarls.

So many times we are just like Tiger when it comes to the devil. We cower beneath him while he plays havoc with our lives. And even if we don't say it, we live in a mode that goes something like this: "Oh, please, sir, kind sir, Mr. Devil, sir. Oh, please don't hurt me, sir, kind sir." We quiver in our boots at the thought of Satan and his army, and we live in defeat because we have not been taught just how strong the victory is we have with the presence of Jesus Christ in our hearts and lives.

Please don't misunderstand me. I am not saying that Satan isn't a powerful being. He is. And if we face him in our own strength, we have no authority and no power. There is no way we'll ever defeat him. But as Christians we do not face him in our own strength. We face him in the power and authority given to us through Jesus Christ our Lord. According to John, "greater is he that is in you, than he that is in the world" (1 John 4:4, KJV).

We don't have to beg the Lord for power. He makes it readily available to us for daily life and spiritual warfare. When our faith in Him is firm and resolute, He gives us His power to defeat the enemy.

Part of the reason our faith in God can be far from firm is because we have more faith in what the devil is doing than what God can do. We attribute as much authority to Satan as we do to God. In other words, we view Satan as an evil god, with all the powers that God the Creator has and all the insight and knowledge that He has. But the truth is, Satan is a being, created by God, equal only to other created beings such as Michael the archangel or the angel Gabriel. He is not God's equal.

Satan is not omnipresent, omnipotent, or omniscient. Only God is present everywhere at the same time. Only He has all power. And only He knows everything. Satan does not. Now the devil is more wily than we are. "Your enemy the devil prowls around like a roaring lion looking for someone to devour" (1 Peter 5:8). He is not a foe to be taken lightly. But he is *not* an evil god. Furthermore, he possesses only the territory in our lives that we give him through allowing his "stuff" into our hearts and homes or through generational sins or bondage that we are blind to and that we have not broken.

Satan's Stuff

In former generations there was a high stress in many denominations on the things Christians shouldn't do or participate in. Movies, music, and books that featured anti-Christian themes were preached against, and people who wanted to live holy lives shunned godless entertainment. Unfortunately, some of these people went too far and created strict, legalistic rules that really had less to do with holy living and more to do with churches controlling their members.

The devil is

not threatened by

weak believers.

I believe that as a reaction to such legalism there are those who have gone too far in the other direction and are giving Satan footholds in their lives by their lack of standards. Today there seems to be less and less concern over the music we habitually listen to, the movies we regularly watch, or the choices in books and other such entertainment. Despite the rigid or unbalanced views that may have been present in the past, God still calls us to live a holy life and continues to ask us to remove everything from our lives that is out of alignment with His standard of holiness.

That's not to say that there aren't some good, clean love songs that are fine to listen to. It's not to say there aren't some decent, fine movies that are great to see or that there aren't wholesome books available. In the past, people made the mistake of "throwing out the baby with the bath water," so to speak. Since some movies were bad, then none were allowed. Since some secular music was not in line with the Bible, then all secular music would "send you to hell." Since some books were evil, then all secular books were banned. This is not balanced. But neither is it balanced to allow books, movies, or music in our lives that take the name of the Lord in vain, encourage idolatry or adultery, or glamorize any number of other sins.

When we regularly bathe our minds in such, we are opening our hearts and homes to Satan. Therefore, we resign territory to him that will ensure our spiritual defeat and the loss of power in our prayer life. It's hard to rebuke and bind Satan when you are up to your knees in his stuff.

Other things Satan uses to claim territory are symbols from his camp. It's important to Christians to educate themselves and understand what these symbols and items are. When we bring into our homes or carry on our person things that are under God's curse, we are assuring Satan of victory in our lives. In the Bible, time and time again, God told His people to shun evil. 1 Thessalonians 5:22 bluntly states, "Avoid every kind of evil."

In the Old Testament there was a reason God told His people to purge themselves and the land of Canaan of any of the pagan idols and images. That's because these items have served as tools of dark worship, represent the manifestation of evil, and are detrimental to the Christian experience. Things like Ouija boards, witch dolls, the skull and crossbones, or any other cultic or demonic imagery should be evil in the eyes of the believer. When we allow these items on our clothing or in our homes, we are as good as saying, "Come on, devil. Walk right in. And while you're at it, bring a whole legion of your friends along with you." It's up to us as believers to listen to the voice of God. When He impresses on us that an item shouldn't be in our home, then we should remove it. If something mysteriously troubles you, then it might very well be God's spirit in conflict with the spirit that particular item or symbol represents.

I'm not talking about some paranoid, fear-filled, knee-jerk reaction that causes us to lie awake at night, terrified that there might be things in our home we don't know about that will allow the devil access to our lives. If something is in our lives that God does not want there, He will be faithful in letting us know. We don't need to live in a paranoid stupor about every item we possess and everything that happens.

I had an acquaintance who once said, "The devil is just all over me today. I'm dropping everything. He's making me drop everything." I thought, *No, you have the "dropsy's." It has nothing to do with the devil.* Some people blame the devil for things he couldn't care less about and live in a world of fear that's not healthy for anyone.

But blaming the devil for every stumbling block in life is just as unbalanced as denying that he and his legions do exist and are panting for every opportunity to destroy our homes, our peace, and our relationship with the Lord. It's detrimental to our spiritual well-being not to recognize that there are some symbols and elements from the Satanic camp that should not be in a Christian's home.

My husband and I have chosen not to allow our kids to have clothing or accessories with the skull and crossbones on them, because this symbol represents evil. Granted, all poisonous substances such as rust remover have skulls and crossbones on them as well. Does that mean I need to throw out my rust remover? Absolutely not! That is ridiculous.

While the skull and crossbones do represent evil in certain contexts, they are also the universal symbol for poison as well. It is appropriate in that context.

The point is, we must be balanced yet cautious. I recall years ago seeing a painting of the devil hanging in someone's living room. I remember, even as a child, getting the creeps from that painting. It doesn't take a Greek scholar to know that such satanic and demonic images have no place in the lives of believers. And when we allow them in our lives, we are allowing Satan a foothold to our hearts and homes.

I recall going to a seminar on spiritual warfare. The director, Nathan Covington, was listing some of the things in our current culture that reflect demonic life. No one had to tell my husband and me that the list of symbols was not appropriate for our home. The Holy Spirit had already made us aware of nearly every item on his list. We had not encountered the other items.

If we listen to the voice of God, He will guide us in all things that are pleasing to Him. But too many times we are not in tune with Him and are living as halfway Christians. According to Corrie ten Boom, "It is dangerous to live as a halfway Christian in this age filled with darkness, chaos, and hopelessness. In the center of a hurricane there is absolute quiet and peace. There is no safer place than in the center of the will of God."[1]

If this chapter has made you aware of how important it is to remove Satan's junk from your life, and the Holy Spirit is bringing things to mind, then have faith in His voice. Discard what He shows you is evil. For a detailed list of some of the items that are from the enemy's camp, see Appendix One.

Satan's Footholds

Another area where we let Satan into our lives is in the footholds he gains in our hearts. Often these come through generational issues that are passed from grandparents to parents and from parents to children. Satan likes nothing more than for Christians to live in denial that these issues are present. As long as we deny the issues, he and his army can continue to entrench themselves in these strongholds. These generational issues can include emotional wounds that were passed down from generation to generation. Often this occurs in the form of patterns of verbal, physical, or spiritual abuse that leave gaping wounds in the soul. Satan loves to camp in those wounds.

A friend of mine, Heidi Tracht, told me that she views our hearts like a giant boulder. In that boulder are small cavities that have been carved out. These cavities are often the result of emotional wounds or generational sins. And these cavities are the areas Satan and his team place their claws in. They remain entrenched in our hearts for decades.

Just as God calls us to remove Satan's "stuff" from our lives, so He calls us to have the courage to break out of denial and shatter generational sin cycles while praying for emotional healing when needed. According to Stormie Omartian, "We all need deliverance at one time or another. That's because no matter how spiritual we are, we're still made of flesh. And no matter how perfectly we live, we still have an enemy who is trying to erect strongholds of evil in our lives. God wants us free from everything that binds, holds, or separates us from Him."[2]

Hour of Power in the Shower

Once I began to deeply realize the truths already stated in this chapter, I made a decision to daily strategize for spiritual offense. I made a conscious choice to take the steps that would stop me from being in a defensive position while the devil tried to gain ground and defeat me. Rather, I decided to be the one purposefully gaining ground through the power of Jesus and letting the devil know that "no weapon forged against [me] will prevail" (Isaiah 54:17). This led me to develop what I call my "hour of power in the shower." First, understand that I don't spend an entire hour in the shower every day. However, my routine begins in the shower and continues the entire time I'm putting on my makeup, fixing my hair, and getting dressed.

We as believers have the

authority to defeat the devil in

the power of Christ as we arm

and protect ourselves with our

knowledge of His Word.

Once I set foot in the shower, I know it's time to claim my day and my life, my family and our ministry for victory in Jesus and to bind the devil and his imps. In doing this, I recognize that my victory over Satan has already been fought for and won. All I have to do is claim it daily and daily bind him. In Matthew 18:18 Jesus states, "I tell you the truth, whatever you bind on earth will be bound in heaven, and whatever you loose on earth will be loosed in heaven." So many times we don't take this scripture to heart and don't stand on its authority. But when we willfully choose to bind Satan in our lives, we are living this verse.

Every day of my life starts with such a prayer. I pray out loud on purpose, because, as already mentioned, the devil cannot read my thoughts. I want him and his army to know I'm up and taking my stand against him. I start out by pleading the blood of Jesus and applying the blood of Jesus upon every member of our immediate family: myself, my husband, our son and daughter. I also pray that the Lord would send His guardian angels to protect us and put His hedge of protection around us. I call each of us by name and pray this prayer over each of us. From there I pray for our property, for the congregation of our church, for my husband and me as pastors, for the church property, and for any extended family members He has laid upon my heart.

Once I firmly establish before God that we are all covered by the blood and that God's protection is upon us, I start kicking Satan around. I say something like, "Satan, I bind you over my husband by the power of Jesus and the name of Jesus and the blood of Jesus. I bind any demons you have assigned to him. I bind any powers or principalities you have assigned to him. I bind any pitfalls you have planned for him and any plans or schemes you have formed against him. I bind you from his past, his present, and his future, and I claim God's healing and anointing and power upon his past and present and future. I bind any generational strongholds you have used against him or plan to use against him. I bind you, Satan, from his sexual purity, and I bind any temptations you have planned for him." When praying for my son and daughter, I include a prayer for their future mates as well. I often close with something like *Dear Jesus, remove temptation from them and keep them far from temptation.*

It's important that we not only ask the Lord to help us withstand any attacks from the devil but also ask Him to remove temptation from us and our families. According to Bruce Wilkinson,

> In my experience, most Christians seem to pray solely for strength to endure temptations—for victory over the attacks of our raging adversary, Satan. Somehow we don't think to ask God simply to keep us away from temptation and keep the devil at bay in our lives. But in the model prayer Jesus gave his followers, nearly a quarter of its fifty words ask for deliverance: "And do not lead us into temp-

tation, But deliver us from the evil one" (Matthew 6:13 NKJV). Without temptation we would not sin.[3]

By praying this way, I turn my getting-ready time every morning into a spiritual war zone. And I have seen results that you would not believe! Strongholds have been broken. Deliverances have been orchestrated. Bondages have been dissolved. The power of Jesus Christ has been unleashed in our lives on a new and amazing level. Any time I face a difficult situation, now, instead of stewing over it or worrying about it, I immediately begin this type of praying—binding Satan and claiming God's victory and power. It's astounding how God moves and difficult situations are turned for the better, sometimes within the hour, sometimes overnight. Granted, I've seen situations take longer to unravel, but God's timing is always perfect. He is faithful, and I never cease to be amazed at the victories that unfold.

When we take a stand against the devil through the power that God has given us, we are stepping into the supernatural realm with Jesus as our conqueror and coming forth victorious through Him, His power, and His shed blood. According to Evelyn Christenson,

> Recently, an occult high priest was quoted in our local newspaper. He said that the churches of America had given up the supernatural. They don't deal in the supernatural—they just deal in plans and programs and social action. He said that every human being is created

with a supernatural vacuum, and since Christians aren't doing anything in the realm of the supernatural, he feels that witchcraft is a reasonable substitute for Christianity. Can we still have the supernatural in our churches? I think we can, for effectual, fervent prayer is capable of producing supernatural results.[4]

When Satan sees that Christians don't recognize or refuse to recognize that we really are not fighting "against flesh and blood, but against the rulers, against the authorities, against the powers of this dark world and against the spiritual forces of evil in the heavenly realms" (Ephesians 6:12), then he knows that he has already won the battle. There's no contest. In any sporting event if one team doesn't show up, the other team is the victor. Likewise, when we just don't show up on the spiritual battlefield, we're passively forfeiting to Satan. God wins every battle—but we need to *show up* for battle!

You might be thinking, *This sounds like a lot of work! I would really rather coast and not worry about it.* Well, it *is* a lot of work. And frankly, there are days I would really rather coast and not think about it, too. There are days my mind wants to wander off to all manner of unimportant things or dwell upon who might have gotten on my nerves or on this or that. But then I find myself stewing over things I should be turning over to the Lord. The longer I stew, the more likely Satan will use the situation against me. Yes, it's work to play spiritual offense. But since when is anything that is of any worth easy? And what is more important than the spiritual success of ourselves, our families, and our ministries?

God has impressed upon me that I have no business letting my guard down. The minute I do, Satan will be there to kill and destroy. And frankly, I cringe to think of other Christians—especially those in ministry—who don't take spiritual warfare seriously. We must daily "put on the full armor of God so that [we] can take [our] stand against the devil's schemes" (Ephesians 6:11). It takes determination and action to daily put on spiritual armor and report for duty. It means we have to connect with God and keep Him and His agenda as the central focus of our lives.

Evelyn Christenson writes,

One day my husband walked out of the sanctuary of our church and encountered our custodian fairly dripping with perspiration. He was a giant of a Christian, but was gradually losing his ability to think and work effectively because of hardening of the arteries. As my husband saw him struggling with the vacuum cleaner, he looked down, and there lying on the floor was the plug. The dear man had vacuumed the whole auditorium and didn't have the plug in the outlet!

Isn't that what happens to many of us? We work, we pull, we struggle, and we plan until we're utterly exhausted, but we have forgotten to plug in to the source

Christians are supposed not

merely to endure change,

nor even to profit by it,

but to cause it.

—Harry Emerson Fosdick

of power. And that source of power is prayer—the "effectual fervent prayer" of a righteous person that avails much.[5]

Are you plugged in and ready to claim the power?

5

The Freedom

~⁓~

If the Son sets you free,
you will be free indeed
(John 8:36).

◦ I met Shirley Porter after having heard about her for weeks. She is the daughter of a dear lady who attends our church whom I fondly refer to as my queen. Like her mother, Shirley emits an air of quiet eloquence that reminds me of a woman who has graduated with honors from the most stringent and finest finishing school. But there's much more to Shirley than her regal graces. As she played the piano in our church, I also sensed a spiritual depth in her that comes only to those who have sacrificed all in pursuit of Christ.

I knew there had to be a story behind Shirley's spiritual depth. Soon I began to peace together the account of a gifted son who had tragically committed suicide after his ship was bombed in May 1987. When Iran "accidentally" fired two missiles on the *USS Stark*, the event made national news. One of the missiles exploded and killed thirty-seven of the one hundred twenty men on board. According to Shirley,

My son Tim was asleep when it happened. He awoke to screams and fire and water. His best friend came to him bleeding and crying, but in the confusion Tim lost sight of him. Another man helped him get his oxygen mask on and they started climbing to the top deck. The man who helped him stepped on a live wire and died in Tim's arms. Tim climbed on and was in the water before he realized that what they had thought were stairs to go up to the deck to safety was in actuality the hole the missile had come through. Of the seven who went into the water, only five survived. Tim's best friend was never found. Tim clung with three others to a small life raft. For eleven and a half hours he prayed for light to come so they could be found. Of all the horrors of that night, the one thing that stood uppermost in his mind was that he could not save his friend.

Quite simply, Tim never got over it. He was diagnosed with post traumatic stress syndrome and given a medical discharge. For the next three years he never slept without nightmares, had recurring flashbacks, would try to come out of it and fail, try and fail, and finally entered the hospital because he knew he was suicidal. They just did not watch him closely enough.[1]

Like any mother, Shirley was devastated after the loss of her son, but through the miraculous process of seeking God, she found the freedom to embrace life again and live fully for Christ. Shirley Porter's personal testimony is a living example of the liberty available to all who are willing to embrace the author of freedom:

And so I came also, asking my questions, at times angry, at times complaining, seemingly always hurting. There were times when I would weep before the Lord, mourning in such intensity, longing to see my son, to hear his voice, to reach out and touch him and I would beseech the Father, saying, "Lord, I cannot bear it," and He would come in great comfort and I could be still in His peace.

There were other times when I would cry out in agony before the Lord because of my longing to see my son, to hear his voice, to reach out and touch him, and I would pray, "O Lord, I cannot bear it," and the sky would be brass. It was as if my prayers went no higher than the ceiling, and it seemed that all I had believed in and stood on for so many years was a mockery, for I felt nothing. Only despair. Just blackness. And it was in those times that I simply endured and began the process of choosing to believe. I chose to believe in His ultimate sovereignty and His goodness, to hang onto His promises, to try to trust. I have quite literally stood on His Word.

So it was there in those blackest of times, I began to make the choices to believe. Not belief based on what I sensed or felt or even what my mind would hurl at me. I would simply cry, "Lord, I believe; help Thou my unbelief." And the day came when I knew with the certainty that only the Lord gives that while He was there when I sensed His presence, He was the most powerfully and awesomely there when I felt nothing but blackness. "Where can I go from Thy Spirit or where can I flee from Thy presence? If I ascend to Heaven, behold Thou art there. If I make my bed in Sheol, behold Thou art there. If I take the wings of the dawn, if I dwell in the remotest part of the sea, even there Thy hand will lead me. If I say, 'Surely the darkness will overwhelm me and the light around me will be night. Even the darkness is not dark to Thee and the night is as bright as the day. Darkness and light are alike to Thee.'"

So as I began to try to trust Him, to try to make choices of simply believing what His Word says, I began to understand deeply the great foundation upon which I stood. He began to show me in His Word and through His body specific ways to grow. And I began to pray, "Search me, O Lord, and know my heart and see if there be any hurtful way in me." How can He heal me when I am not even aware of the areas of my life that need healing? And how can I be aware unless His Spirit shows me? Oh, I can be introspective of myself, and the enemy of my soul will be my accuser and condemn me for my weaknesses and failures until I will avoid even the appearance of examining myself, but that is not what His Word says. The Psalmist said to the Lord, "Search me." For when His spirit searches our hearts, He knows when we are ready to hear and when we can hear His word of examination. And so, as I let His Spirit search my heart, He began to show me the broken places of my own life that had been ignored for so long; some of those areas of my life were broken because of my own sin that I could not see. Other deeply broken places of my life were there because of the sins of others that had been perpetrated upon me. But you know, regardless of where we are in life and the mental or emotional suffering or difficulties that we bear, the steps of healing are still the same. Jesus knows our frame; He knows every circumstance, every cry of our heart, and the steps of healing are still the same.

We so often think the Cross and the cleansing blood of Christ is for our salvation, and yes, it is—it most wonderfully is—but it is also our way of life and our way forward from where we are or where we have been. He will show us if our turmoil is rooted in our own sin or the sins of others, or if it is a circumstance or situation in life that He has expressly commanded. But the healing is always the same. If it is our own sin, He will so gently show us and bring us to repentance and His blood will cleanse and completely heal. If it is caused by the sins of others, again it is the Cross that is our hope, for He will gently lead us to forgiveness and a releasing of our own bitterness so that healing can come.

So it is that healing began in those areas of my life. As I came to Him in repentance of my own sin and in becoming aware of how the sins of others had affected me, the cleansing blood of Christ not only brought forgiveness to me but started the healing process in the wounded places caused by others' sins. Did I bear the consequences of those sins over the years? Yes, I did, and I grieved and mourned over lost opportunities and wrong choices that affected not only me but also my family. But as Oswald Chambers has so beautifully said, "Let the past sleep but let it sleep on the bosom of Christ. Leave the irreparable past with Him and step out into he irresistible future with Christ."

The beauty and wonder are that as He day by day, week by week, month by month and year by year continued to try to teach me more of His ways, I began again to be able to truly praise Him, to smile again, to laugh again, to know He has a purpose yet for me, to understand more deeply the pain and suffering of others, to know how to comfort. . . .

These are just small portions of the many lessons that He is trying still to teach me as I seek to walk with Him. Have I found the answers for pain and suffering? If I had, surely they would have been on the best-seller list by now, and I would be signing autographs to its pages. No, quite simply there are some things for which there are no earthly answers. But as I have sat at His feet and tried to learn to abandon myself to Him, His Spirit began to show me what I call the outskirts of His holiness, the depth of His sovereignty, His never-failing faithfulness, and His fathomless love.[2]

Preparing for Freedom

Before an army goes to battle, it prepares for the task. Each soldier is required to go through boot camp. Some are

The only way we can be of use to

God is to let Him take us through

the crooks and crannies of our

own characters. It is astounding

how ignorant we are about

ourselves! We do not know envy

when we see it, or laziness, or

pride. Jesus reveals to us all that

this body has been harboring

before His grace began to work.

How many of us have learned

to look in with courage.

—Oswald Chambers[3]

enlisted in specialty training. The weapons are secured and loaded with artillery. And in modern times, all avenues of technology are researched and employed. The enemy is recognized, analyzed, and categorized. The side who is the most prepared and the most focused is usually the side who wins.

So it goes with our quest for spiritual freedom. As an army prepares for battle, so we must be willing to prepare for freedom. For the Christian, that preparation happens when we are willing to put in time in "spiritual boot camp." This is the place where we finally get on our face before God, as Shirley Porter described. Some people arrive there by a soul-deep hunger for an experience with God that "Grandma had." Others arrive through a doorway marked tragedy; others through the pathway of hardship.

According to Stormie Omartian,

> God uses difficult times to purify us. The Bible says, "Since Christ suffered for us in the flesh, arm yourselves also with the same mind, for he who has suffered in the flesh has ceased from sin" (1 Peter 4:1 NKJV). This means our suffering during difficult times will burn sin and selfishness out of our lives. God allows suffering to happen so that we will learn to live for Him and not for ourselves. So that we will pursue His will and not our own. It's not pleasant at the time, but God's desire is "that we may be partakers of His holiness" (Hebrews 12:10,

NKJV). He wants us to let go of the things we lust after and cling to what is most important in life—Him.[4]

Whatever the avenue, those who have trod into true freedom have burst into it after a season of intense seeking, waiting, and consecration from their side with healing and purging from God's side. The freedom God grants often involves the breaking of bondage from the past as well as from sin—our own and that which has been committed against us. Too many times we want to hang onto these beasts in our lives because they propel us forward in a continuing cycle of self-focus that feels so right because it has served us so well. The sad thing is that so many people are born into a generational sin or bondage, and they never even realize they're oppressed. Only by our willingness to boldly encounter a holy God and allow Him to examine the crooks and crannies of our hearts do we begin to taste the freedom that He has to offer the consecrated soul.

> *Once I was bound by sin's galling fetters;*
> *Chained like a slave, I struggled in vain.*
> *But I received a glorious freedom*
> *When Jesus broke my fetters in twain.*
>
> *Glorious freedom!*
> *Wonderful freedom!*
> *No more in chains of sin I repine!*
> *Jesus, the glorious Emancipator—*
> *Now and forever He shall be mine.*[5]

Our Side: Consecration

Once we have accepted Christ as our Savior and begun our journey of seeking Him and waiting upon Him, He soon shows us that there is a difference between surrendering to Jesus and consecrating ourselves to Him. Only through a full consecration do we find complete freedom. Understand that we *surrender* to Jesus when He saves us. When any Christian seriously seeks Him, He ultimately asks us to willingly set ourselves apart to be used wholly by Him. This is the act of consecration. For instance, when a criminal gets caught in a crime and leaves with the police, he or she is surrendering. He or she is not consecrating himself to law and order.

Second Corinthians 7:1 states, "Let us purify ourselves from everything that contaminates body and spirit, perfecting holiness out of reverence for God." According to Stormie Omartian, "Holiness means separating yourself from the world. This doesn't mean you head for the hills, isolate yourself, and never speak to a nonbeliever. It means your heart detaches from the world's value system. You, instead, value the things God values above all else."[6] The things of God are the heartbeat of the one who is fully consecrated to Him.

It is important to realize that an unsaved person can't consecrate to God and fulfill Paul's command to "purify ourselves—perfecting holiness out of reverence for God." Since a saved person is already surrendered, then he or she is called upon to present himself or herself totally to God for His use when or where He likes, however He wishes. Through this process, we yield to God our possessions, talents, ambitions, loved ones, future, ourselves, our pasts, and our right to control our own destiny or anything we attempt to accomplish. This is no means an easy task. Some great people of faith had tremendous struggles with this, but they didn't become great until they consecrated all to God.

Consecrating ourselves is the human side of holiness. When Paul uses the term "perfecting holiness," he is implying that the process has begun. And so it goes when we are saved; we receive the witness of his Holy Spirit at work in our hearts. "Perfecting holiness" doesn't mean we have to finish something God started and can't finish. God does what we can't. He changes us inside through the fullness of His Holy Spirit. Our consecration must involve a willful purifying of body and spirit as far as we know and are able. The perfecting of holiness requires a thorough cleansing from the defilement of body and spirit. This includes everything from our attitudes to our habits. Anything in our lives contrary to living a holy life must be dealt with and released.

Understand that God will not force us to release anything. Furthermore, He cannot and will not release *for* us. In our journey to freedom, there are some things God requires us to do; releasing is one of them. While it's very attractive to embrace the notion that God does everything and we just

sit in a spiritual trance and aren't asked to do a thing, it's not
realistic or Scriptural.

Freedom from all the carnal affections;
Freedom from envy, hatred, and strife;
Freedom vain and worldly ambitions;
Freedom from all that saddened my life!

Glorious freedom!
Wonderful freedom!
No more in chains of sin I repine!
Jesus, the glorious Emancipator—
Now and forever He shall be mine.[7]

Crossing the Jordan

The Old Testament offers an excellent example of what
consecration is and the effects it brings. After wandering in
the wilderness for forty long years, the children of Israel finally got to a point where they were willing to claim the
Promised Land. They sent spies into the land who came back
with a positive report. They believed that the Lord was giving them the whole land because "all the people are melting
in fear because of us" (Joshua 2:24).

Before the children of Israel crossed the Jordan River,
Joshua said, "Consecrate yourselves, for tomorrow the LORD
will do amazing things among you" (Joshua 3:5). Now these
were the same group of people who had been grumbling and

griping and totally self-centered. They thought about one thing—themselves—and were ready to complain if everything didn't go their way. But Joshua told them it was time to get their minds off themselves and on God and to direct their energies to the things of God. He was telling them to consecrate to the point of getting rid of anything that harmed their relationship with God and to embrace all that supported their faith.

Think about the order of what Joshua said. First, he told the Israelites to consecrate themselves and *then* the Lord would do amazing things. Before they could enjoy the Promised Land, their consecration must be complete. Likewise, before God's Spirit can have complete control of us, before we can taste His freedom, we must be willing to consecrate all we are to Him. Don't mistake surrender for consecration.

The children of Israel were about to begin a new experience. They went from slavery in Egypt to bondage in the desert and had lived in defeat for forty years. But God was ready to change all that. The same is true with us. So many times we live in bondage when God wants to give us freedom—but complete freedom comes only through the doorway marked "consecration."

The children of Israel had many sacred traditions. However, the ark of the covenant transcended tradition and was actually a special vessel that symbolized the presence of a holy God. The ark represented the holy of holies and went with the Israelites wherever they traveled. Normally, the ark was carried behind the children of Israel. But when they went across the Jordan, the Israelites changed the position of the ark of the covenant (v. 11) and placed it in front of them. They essentially moved God to the lead and said, "We will follow you to freedom."

In their lives, the ark represented the powerful presence of God in their camp. In our lives, the ark is symbolic of Jesus Christ. When God asks us to consecrate ourselves unto Him, He must be placed in the lead in our lives. We follow Him to freedom.

The Israelites had been aimlessly wandering for years, but all that changed when they began following the ark. That's when they encountered God's power! He miraculously parted the Jordan just as He had parted the Red Sea, and they walked across to freedom on dry ground. Likewise, only when we place Christ in the lead will we experience God's power to set us free from our past, our failures, our pain, and usher us into our own promised land. But the first step is consecration!

Too many times, Jesus is treated like a passenger or a hitchhiker or a mere companion we encounter in life. But when we relinquish the lead of our lives totally to Him, we are pronouncing complete reliance upon Him. In doing this, we commit ourselves to obey what we already know to be

God's will. A significant portion of His will is stated in the Bible. God expects us to adhere to His general will before guiding us in His specific will.

There's so much freedom in knowing that if God wants me to do something He will orchestrate the whole thing. Doors will open. Circumstances will line up. All I have to do is be willing to step forward with Him in the lead. I don't have to fight the battles; He fights them for me. I don't have to prove myself; He proves me. I don't have to worry about circumstances like mighty, rushing rivers that are too big for me to cross. He miraculously parts the waters and ushers me through. My primary calling is to consecrate myself to Him and merely follow where He leads. If that's into a situation that seems too big for me and makes me uncomfortable, He will be there. He will be my strength, my wisdom.

That's exactly what He did for the children of Israel. Imagine being one of the priests holding the ark while two to three million people hurried across the dry river bed. Even though the water "piled up in a heap a great distance away," (v. 16), I'm sure the priests were eager to see the last person marching through. When the consecrated heart is in the middle of a mess and is ready to cry, "Dear Lord— block the water! I'm still in the river bed!" as long as we have the "ark of the covenant" there with us, we have the power of Jesus. Isaiah 43:1-2 states, "Fear not . . . When you pass through the waters, I will be with you." There's great freedom in knowing that no matter what life throws at us, He is there with us, and our problems become *His* problems. Even when we face failures because of our own choices, He is there to pick us up and redeem the situation.

When we commit to following Jesus, there's such freedom in knowing that He prepares our way. As Shirley Porter mentioned, sometimes we may believe He's not there. But those are the times we can look back and see that He was there even more so, holding us up, as we obeyed. Before He parted the waters for the Israelites, they had to put their feet into the water. He required their obedience. So it is with us. There are situations when He requires that we have "wet feet" first. God didn't need to part the waters until they had shown the faith to obey and step in.

Interestingly enough, this was the same river where Jesus was baptized and the Spirit descended upon Him like a dove. The Jordan River is a scriptural metaphor for the line of demarcation between bondage and freedom, wilderness and the land of milk and honey. We are called to obey Joshua's command to consecrate ourselves as well as Paul's admonishment to "purify ourselves . . . perfecting holiness out of reverence for God." Remember, the children of Israel didn't receive the freedom of the promised land until they consecrated themselves to all that was holy.

Freedom from fear with all of its torments;
Freedom from care with all of its pain;

Freedom in Christ, my blessed Redeemer—
He who has rent my fetters in twain.

Glorious freedom!
Wonderful freedom!
No more in chains of sin I repine!
Jesus, the glorious Emancipator—
Now and forever He shall be mine.[8]

God's Side: Healing and Purging

Earlier I used the term "Spiritual Boot Camp" as a description for the place where our freedom begins. As much as I would love to soften this description, it fits the scenario all too well. We live in an age of comfort and effortless gratification, from instant potatoes to remote controls. We often approach our spiritual journey in the same mentality—as if God will give us an easy journey to freedom and intimacy with Him with very little effort on our parts. Unfortunately, it just doesn't work that way. He has given His all to us, and He asks us to consecrate all we are to Him.

None of this is to say that our salvation or relationship with God is based on our works. Ephesians 2:8-9 states, "It is by grace you have been saved, through faith—and this not from yourselves, it is the gift of God—not by works, so that no one can boast."

But we must understand that what we do does matter. We do reap what we sow. "Do not be deceived: God cannot be mocked. A man reaps what he sows" (Galatians 6:7).

When we invest time, energy, and effort into our relationship with the Lord and make ourselves available for Him to invest time, energy, and effort into us, we have entered into a holy partnership that leads us into true freedom. Only when we totally place ourselves in the hands of a holy God can He truly begin the process of healing and purging.

Healing

As I have traveled the United States and spoken to thousands of people, more often than not I have encountered throngs who were battling issues of which they were desperate to be free. I never cease to be amazed at how often these issues involve the past. The stories I have been told often involve tragic pasts that the person had no control over. Like the children of Israel, these people are wandering around in a state of spiritual numbness, not sure which direction they should go. But even when this is the case, those who consecrate themselves find that God is willing and ready to bring the healing that is needed. All we have to do is immerse ourselves into the waters of His presence and wait for Him to complete the healing.

I would love to tell you that I haven't been there on this issue, but I can't. As a survivor of sexual abuse, I know what bondage to the past feels like. I know the devastation of being chained by recurring memories and shame. I understand the subconscious coping mechanisms that so many survivors of abuse fall into without even realizing it. I also know that God is faithful to heal and deliver us from our own sin as well as sins committed against us. But it does take time.

According to John Killinger,

A way of praying is by blessing your memories. The idea is to evoke your memories one by one, holding them before God for a few moments and thanking him for them as you do. Painful memories as well as pleasant ones. They too are part of the fabric of your existence. They help to make you what you are today. And if God accepts you as you are, then you can accept your memories as they are. Actually this is a kind of therapy, for it is a positive way of dealing with parts of your past you have never been able to fully accept. It will deepen your faith by letting you see the panorama of years under the loving care of the heavenly Father. The result will be a greater steadiness in future times of crisis and pain. This too shall pass, you will think, *and become part of the history of my life. It is good to live, and to give thanks to God!*[9]

So many times people are afraid of their memories and suppress them deep in their minds. While I understand how painful it is to relive certain aspects of the past, I also know there is much healing in pondering memories in God's presence. This is an unraveling process that God uses in undoing the effects of harmful events in our lives and untangling our spirits from the chains that these events wrap us in.

While I would never have chosen to be sexually abused, I can thank God for the depth and wisdom I gleaned from having to hang onto Him in order to survive the aftermath. The deeper the wounds, the deeper His healing and love must go and the greater the opportunity for us to grow in understanding His grace. Blessing our memories means we give them up to God and ask Him to fulfill scripture: "We know that in all things God works for the good of those who love him, who have been called according to his purpose" (Romans 8:28).

Understand that Satan is the author of lies and bondage. He wants to undo every inch of freedom God brings into our lives by hurling us back into bondage. This is exactly what happened to the children of Israel when they exchanged the slavery of Egypt for the spiritual bondage in the dessert. It took forty years before they broke into true freedom. Don't allow this same scenario to happen to you! While you embrace your freedom and deliverance, accept that you will have to guard it, or it will be stolen from you.

This regression often happens in our minds when we begin a shame-based dwelling upon our past failures or the things that have been done to us. We must not dwell on every thought that comes into our minds but rather allow the Holy Spirit to take our thoughts captive and tear down every stronghold.

Understand that perpetual dwelling upon the past is different than lifting your memories to the Lord as you meditate before Him. Dwelling upon the past involves a continual replaying of past events in a stream-of-consciousness state of being that forever keeps your focus on your past and yourself and off God. If we have experienced a tragic past, it's so easy to stay in an insecure, victim mode with a complete self-focus. Interestingly enough, the person who has an arrogant level of self-esteem and the person who has low self-esteem both are self-focused. The arrogant person is focused upon how much better he or she is than everyone else, while the person with low self-esteem is focused on how much worse he or she is than everyone else. Still, both are focused upon the self. And this is where Satan would keep us trapped: focused upon ourselves, our unjust past, and our failures, rather than the freedom found in Christ.

According to Corrie ten Boom, "So many people are like tightrope walkers. In one hand they have a sack filled with their unjust past, in the other hand a sack filled with the anticipated future. They are balancing between hope and despair. That attitude is wrong. Have you the Holy Spirit, or has the Holy Spirit you?"[11]

When we truly consecrate ourselves to God and allow the Holy Spirit to have all of us, He is then free to begin the

The true end of prayer is

not getting from God,

but giving ourselves

to God.

—Charles L. Allen[10]

healing process. Psalm 147:3 reads, "He heals the broken-hearted and binds up their wounds." Without our willingness to give the Great Physician full control of our hearts, our wounds only fester and deepen, and we never know complete freedom.

Purging

I would like to tell you I love the process of purging, but the very thought makes me wince—and so it is with anyone who has undergone seasons of holy purging. I can honestly testify that I'm thrilled with the effect of purging, because a new depth of freedom is always waiting on the other side. But the process has never been easy or painless.

When soldiers enter boot camp, the sergeant's job is to purge every weakness from their bodies and instill resilience and focus within them. They are taken through weeks of strenuous physical training to ensure that they are strong and ready for the battle. I've never heard one soldier ever say, "Wonderful! I get to do two hundred more sit-ups today! I just love this pain!" No, they groan and strain and think they might die before it's all over. But when they persevere, they are thrilled with the benefits and the results.

So it goes in spiritual boot camp. When we consecrate ourselves to all that is holy, God then begins a purging within us to remove weaknesses from us that will hinder our witness and our labor for His kingdom. Sometimes this purging involves making us aware of and asking us to release sin that we are harboring in our hearts: selfish ambition, vanity, envy, or bad attitudes, just to name a few.

Understand that there is a difference between willful, known sin and missing the mark. The Bible mentions both types of sin. If there is willful, known sin in our lives, God requires that we remove it as part of our consecration. But there are many times we are missing the mark and don't even realize it. This is where God's purging comes in. And it's necessary to allow Him to shine His holy light upon the crevices of our soul in order to purge us of these areas where we are missing the mark. Even if we are unaware that we are trapped by a sin, the result is still bondage.

You might ask, "How can you be unaware of a sin in your life?" Understand that with every past injury we have suffered, there is often a coping mechanism, or sinful behavioral pattern, that good Christian people subconsciously fall into without even realizing it. I have seen people who love the Lord with all they are and desperately want to do His will, manifest all manner of bad behavior without ever understanding the impact they are having on others. There seems to be one set of rules for the way they want to be treated and another set of rules for the way they treat others. When their bad treatment of others backfires on them, they are shocked, because they are totally unconscious of their problems.

For instance, always wanting control of situations can be the results of a carnal heart that is self-focused and consciously wants its own way or else. Or it can be the result of a deeply injured person who unknowingly adopts co-dependency as a means of coping. Co-dependent Christians are as rare as water on a Pacific island. They desperately need praise, approval, and applause but also need to control everything they touch. Furthermore, they surround themselves with "needy" people who will depend upon them. This gives them further control over people. Unfortunately, they are often applauded for helping those in need, when in reality they are creating situations in which others will depend upon them. This does nothing to truly help the needy.*

Always needing control, whether driven by a carnal heart or by an emotional wound, is the antithesis of a life of freedom. Understand that a person can be as pure as snow within his or her heart but still have coping mechanisms due to emotional wounds that God needs to heal and purge. Therefore, submitting ourselves to spiritual boot camp and allowing God to purge us should be a way of life for the consecrated Christian. With every season of purging and healing, the freedom increases. When devout Christians think they are beyond the need of God's purging, they are in a

---

*For a good book on this subject, see *When Pleasing Others Is Hurting You*, by David Hawkins, Harvest House Publishers.

dangerous place and are very likely already manifesting all manner of sinful coping mechanisms, including control issues, which they cannot see and they will not see as long as they refuse the purging process.

When the children of Israel crossed the Jordan, God gave them the assignment to allow Him to purge the land of any impurities through them. In their case, the impurities were represented by people who worshiped pagan Gods. The story of the walls of Jericho tumbling down is but one example of God's purging the land. He wanted no hint of idolatry in their midst. Remember: these were people who had wholly consecrated themselves to God. Nevertheless, God demanded that they allow Him to purge the land, using them as His instruments.

Somewhere in the process, they got busy with life and left pockets of idolatry here and there. Those pockets proved their downfall. Eventually, the worship of pagan gods overtook the Israelites because of their lack of completing the purging process and protecting the land of any further compromise.

So it is with our consecrated hearts. We must be willing to submit ourselves to God's regular purging and not let pride get in the way of our admitting when He has shown us an area where we are unknowingly missing the mark. Then we must be willing to stay on holy guard against the enemy gaining ground in our lives and stealing our freedom and our peace.

> *At the sign of triumph*
> *Satan's host doth flee;*
> *On, then, Christian soldiers,*
> *On to victory!*
> *Hell's foundations quiver*
> *At the shout of praise;*
> *Christians, lift your voices,*
> *Loud your anthems raise!*
> *Onward, Christian soldiers!*
> *Marching as to war,*
> *With the cross of Jesus*
> *Going on before.*[12]

6

The Peace

‿✦‿

Thou wilt keep him in perfect
peace, whose mind is stayed on
thee: because he trusteth in thee
(Isaiah 26:3, KJV).

According to Charles L. Allen,

After Rabbi Liebman wrote his book, *Peace of Mind*, he was swamped with people seeking that peace. His mail was heavy, his telephone rang constantly, people came to his study all day and even to his home at night. He was a kindhearted young man of only thirty-eight years. He tried to help every person and he died in three years, at forty-one. He just couldn't stand the burden. But before he died he said, "I am appalled at the multitudes of people who have never learned to empty their minds."[1]

Tiffany is a woman who struggled with emptying her mind. A large part of the battle involved the fact that her life was filled with people and situations that perpetuated constant problems and compromised her peace on every hand. During her entire adult life, Tiffany stayed in an uptight state without ever realizing it—to the point that she couldn't sleep. She spent over twenty years taking an over-the-counter, non-addictive sleep aid. Ironically, Tiffany took the sleep aid because she believed she had a sleep disorder and never connected her chronic insomnia with the constant upheaval.

Sometimes negative circumstances can become such a part of our lives that we don't even realize how bad they are. We all know the story of the proverbial frog that is placed in a pot of water that is slowly warmed. He gets so used to the gradual increase in temperature that when he realizes it's too hot for him to live, it's too late. He's already "cooked," and he can't jump to safety before he boils.

Such was Tiffany's existence. A series of tragic events in her teen years shattered her spirit and left her in perpetual internal turmoil. Add to that the constant upheaval, attacks, and verbal abuse from other sources—her life and nerves were in a never-ending stretch.

Tiffany had experienced a deep and real peace at age twelve when, as a Christian, she wholly consecrated herself to Christ. She remembers thinking that she was ready to go to heaven if the unbelievable peace she experienced was like heaven. But in just a few short years, that peace was shattered like a mirror struck by a brick. As the images in such a mirror become splintered and distorted, so Tiffany's mind, spirit, and view of life became disjointed.

Nevertheless, she remained a committed Christian and desperately tried to cope with the circumstances that dysfunctional people continued to heap upon her. As a Christian, she erroneously believed that she was setting a "Christlike example" by meekly taking whatever bad treatment people wanted to heap upon her.

And peace? She never thought about peace much. It had been so long since she had tasted it that she had forgotten that there even was a pure peace. Sure, she knew Jesus was the author of peace, and she did experience a certain measure of peace during her prayer time. But the all-encompassing, mind-boggling peace that eludes so many had evaded Tiffany so long that she never expected to experience it.

After years of developing a divine romance with God and His gradual peeling away the scars of abuse and constant turmoil, Tiffany realized God was telling her it was time to take responsibility for the negative situations in her life. She sensed His promptings to begin to place some serious boundaries on those who kept her in a constant state of unrest.

Eventually, Tiffany found the courage to draw those boundaries. She took a break from some relationships. As for others who had verbally abused her for years, she seriously limited communication with them. She stopped giving them the opportunity to explode into her life and hurl insults whenever they chose. Eventually, Tiffany realized that she had been exactly like the frog in warming water and had gradually allowed bad circumstances to heat to the point of almost boiling her alive.

Once the turmoil was no longer in her life, the unbelievable peace she experienced at twelve came back. And that's when she remembered what it had felt like. The peace that "surpasses all understanding" (Philippians 4:7, NKJV) descended upon her heart, mind, spirit, and emotions. The results were as breathtaking as the first glimpse of heaven, and she once again longed for that eternal destiny. For the first time in her adult life Tiffany was able to sleep all night

We seek peace, knowing that

peace is the climate of freedom.

—Dwight D. Eisenhower

without medication. Her constant state of hyperactivity eased. She was free to just "be" with God, to go even deeper into the divine romance, to enjoy once again a little taste of heaven.

The Strategies of Peace

So many times we view peace as a gift rather than a choice. Even though the very existence of peace is a gift from God, attaining it often requires taking certain God-ordained steps that only He dictates per individual situation. If a Christian is not immersed in peace, there is a reason and there is a solution. The reason might involve a spiritual problem, such as fighting a full consecration to God. But often the lack of heavenly peace can be related to circumstances that could be changed through a series of strategic moves that only God knows.

You may be thinking, *Well, you just don't know how difficult my mate is. There's no peace living with that person;* or *You could never understand what I've gone through and how it has devastated me!*

I would probably answer, "Who knows? Maybe I *would* understand." Then maybe you're right, and I wouldn't be able to comprehend it. But whether or not I can fathom your situation isn't the issue. The issue is that God *does* comprehend it!

He sees everything you've been through. He knows all the pain and scars you bear. He senses the anxiety and turmoil that keep your life in an upheaval. And He wanted to extend unbelievable peace to you so badly that He stretched himself out on the Cross so that you might overcome and transcend whatever life has thrown at you.

The issue is—How badly do you want peace? According to Charles L. Allen, "The better you become acquainted with God, the less tensions you feel and the more peace you possess."[2] Do you want peace enough to go deep with God and allow Him to show you what measures you should take to find that peace? Do you want peace enough to implement the specific strategies He shows you as well as general strategies that are clearly written in His Word?

While there are individual strategies for peace for each person and his or her situations in life, there are also *general* strategies that any of us can embrace any time we sense our peace is diminishing or being compromised. Galatians 5:22-23 states, "The fruit of the Spirit is love, joy, peace, patience, kindness, goodness, faithfulness, gentleness and self-control. Against such things there is no law." Clearly, peace is considered a product of the Spirit-filled life. "For in him we live and move and have our being" (Acts 17:28).

In John 14:27 Jesus himself stated, "Peace I leave with you; my peace I give you. I do not give to you as the world gives." The world's peace too often is forced peace and involves such things as nations declaring cease fires out of fear of nuclear attacks; or people who really hate each other living in peace just to satisfy a third party.

The peace Jesus gives comes in spite of circumstances. His peace isn't forced. It's the fruit of the Spirit, which grows in us through the Holy Spirit as He abides within. No circumstance or person can take this peace from us—unless we let them. In situations such as Tiffany's, God can and will direct us to take the necessary measures to reclaim the peace that Satan uses others to destroy. Even when we are going through the darkest valleys of relationships, tragedies, or illnesses, God's powerful peace proves itself steadfast.

Colossians 3:12-15 states, "As God's chosen people, holy and dearly loved, clothe yourselves with compassion, kindness, humility, gentleness and patience. Bear with each other and forgive whatever grievances you may have against one another. Forgive as the Lord forgave you. And over all these virtues put on love, which binds them all together in perfect unity. Let the peace of Christ rule in your hearts, since as members of one body you were called to peace. And be thankful." Notice that Paul tells us to let the peace of Christ "rule" our hearts. The word "rule" is an athletic word used for an umpire. Paul was saying, "Let the peace of God be the umpire of your heart." In a ball game, the umpire has final say. If the umpire makes a call the coach doesn't like, the coach can argue, spit, and kick dirt on him all he wants, but it doesn't do any good. The umpire's call remains. And if a coach or manager or team owner gets too pushy, he or she can be thrown out of the game.

When Paul was imploring us to let the peace of God be our umpire, he was implying a total surrender. So there is no longer a conflict over who is in charge of our lives—no more kicking and screaming and resisting the lordship of Christ. Understand that this peace must be maintained. As already mentioned, it is a gift, but we have to be willing to take the measures necessary to keep it ours.

Rejoice

Paul describes the necessary measures for peace in Philippians 4:4-7—"Rejoice in the Lord always. I will say it again: Rejoice! Let your gentleness be evident to all. The Lord is near. Do not be anxious about anything, but in everything, by prayer and petition, with thanksgiving, present your requests to God. And the peace of God, which transcends all understanding, will guard your hearts and your minds in Christ Jesus." First, Paul pinpoints joy as a source of peace. Notice he tells us to rejoice in the Lord *twice*. Intimacy with Jesus Christ is the source of our joy. It's not in possessions, circumstances, or people.

Sometimes we can place other people as rulers of our hearts without realizing it. This is what happened with Tiffany. When we take ourselves off the throne of our lives, it's important that we don't place another person or persons there instead of God. When we allow people to habitually crash into our lives and destroy our peace, then it's important that we examine to whom we are giving control of our lives. While many well-meaning Christians clearly don't have themselves on the throne of their own hearts, sometimes God is not there either. And sometimes the throne to our hearts has been forcefully seized by overbearing people whom Satan uses to keep us in defeat.

This can come about because people often look in wrong places for joy. The approval of others is just as erroneous a source of joy as depending on circumstances to bring it. When Paul wrote Philippians, he was in prison; he was staring death eye-to-eye. The church was headed for persecution. Paul was facing it firsthand. But Paul continued to rejoice in the Lord.

There are those who solely depend on circumstances for their joy. The problem is, circumstances change! Of course, anybody will be disappointed if his or her daughter's basketball team lost the state championship. Anyone would be devastated from losing his or her mate in a tragic accident. We're all human—not robots. But when we hit dark moments, we can still know an ultimate joy rooted in peace, which transcends all life's ups and downs. The reason Christians can fulfill Paul's admonishment to "rejoice in the Lord always" is because Jesus is always there regardless of the circumstances. We find the ultimate joy in an ever-deepening intimacy with Christ.

Flee Worry

In Philippians 4:6 Paul states, "Do not be anxious about anything," and pinpoints another major source for a lack of peace. Worrying is like a rocking chair. You are flung forward and backward and get nowhere near solving your problems. In his famous quote Robert Frost declares, "The reason why worry kills more people than work does is that more people worry than work." Mahatma Ghandi stated, "There is nothing that wastes the body like worry, and one who has any faith in God should be ashamed to worry about anything whatsoever."

My dear grandmother, who has long since gone to be with Jesus, was a shouting saint, but she was also a chronic worrier. I think she worried about worrying. Unfortunately, most of what she worried about never came about. I say this was unfortunate, because she put so much time into worrying, and it was such a waste of effort. So it is with all of us who worry. Some wise soul once said, "Don't tell me that worry doesn't do any good. I know better. The things I worry about don't happen."

According to Charles L. Allen,

A physician made a study of the matters his patients were afraid of. Forty percent of the fears were over things that never happened. Thirty percent were over past events which were beyond control. Twelve percent were fearful of their health, though their illnesses were imaginary. Ten percent were afraid over the well-being of some loved one.

Only eight percent of the fears of this physician's patients had any real cause which needed attention. Ninety-two percent of their fears were needless.[3]

In Matthew 6:31-34 Jesus hits worry head-on with these words: "Do not worry, saying, 'What shall we eat?' or 'What shall we drink?' or 'What shall we wear?' For the pagans run after all these things, and your heavenly Father knows that you need them. But seek first his kingdom and his righteousness, and all these things will be given to you as well. Therefore do not worry about tomorrow, for tomorrow will worry about itself. Each day has enough trouble of its own."

Worry and anxiety are burdens that God doesn't want us to carry. I wonder how God views chronic worry. Could it be like a slap in His face for us to be filled with anxiety and fear about the future? Perhaps He views it as our telling Him we don't believe His Word when it says He is in charge and He will carry us through—no matter what. The more time we take to walk in intimacy with God, the fewer our worries should be.

A Swedish proverb says, "Worry gives a small thing a big shadow." So when you find your peace being shadowed by worries, follow Paul's advice in Philippians 4:6—"By prayer and petition, with thanksgiving, present your requests to God."

Anytime you slip into a pattern of worry, immediately start praying about it. Pray that the situation will be solved in God's time and God's way, not yours. You can't worry and pray at the same time.

Worry can be a habit that pulls down our hearts and minds and spirits, but prayer is the victor over worry! Worry focuses on the unknown. Prayer awaits answers and leaves the best choice to God. Worry exhausts us. Prayer rejuvenates us, because we tap into the source of all power. Worry dwells on crises. Prayer reaches out to the One who calmed the storm and has the solution to every upheaval.

According to Charles L. Allen,

Most of life for each of us is happy and good. Yet some black spots are certain to appear from time to time. No life can be completely free of sorrows, disappointments and failures. But to keep our minds stayed on those things will take away from us all the joy of living. The Bible says, "For as he thinketh in his heart, so is he . . ." (Proverbs 23:7, KJV). What you think about is the most important factor in determining what your life will be.[4]

Reinhold Niebuhr is famous for what has become the "Serenity Prayer." Claim it as your daily ticket to worry-free peace: "God, give me the serenity to accept things which cannot be changed; Give me the courage to change things

which must be changed; And the wisdom to distinguish one
from the other."

> *When upon life's billows you are tempest-tossed,*
>
> *When you are discouraged, thinking all is lost,*
>
> *Count your many blessings—name them one by one—*
>
> *And it will surprise you what the Lord hath done.*[5]

Be Thankful

Not only are we called to overcome worry and anxiety
with prayer, but we are also called "With thanksgiving, [to]
present your requests to God" (Philippians 4:6). You might
be thinking, *I'm in such turmoil right now, I don't have anything to be thankful for.* Then be thankful that all believers
have access to a God who truly cares and truly listens! After
pondering that one marvelous truth for a while, you will find
that the reasons to be thankful are endless. Someone once
said, "Count your many blessings—name them ton by ton!"

In 1 Thessalonians 5:16-18, Paul encourages readers to
"Be joyful always; pray continually; give thanks in all circumstances, for this is God's will for you in Christ Jesus."
He mentions "all circumstances," whether joyful or sorrow-
ful. This takes a supernatural gratitude that is a gift from
God which comes when a believer's heart is in full submission to God's will. We can choose peace by daily choosing to
find something to thank God for.

My husband and I have recently been introduced to the ministry of Nick Vujicic. Nick is an incredible Christian man who has a worldwide ministry. He speaks to millions of people all over the globe. He encourages many to not give up hope. He is a living example of God taking what most people would view as a tragedy and turning it into something spectacular. For you see, Nick Vujicic was born with no arms or legs. Yet by the power of Jesus, he has overcome. He is living an unbelievable life of globally proclaiming the Good News.

On the days you truly struggle for something to be thankful for, thank God that you have arms and legs. Even if you only have one arm or one leg, at least you have one! All Nick Vujicic has is what he calls his "little chicken drumstick"—one appendage off his right hip that vaguely resembles a fish fin with a big toe. He testifies that when he got over feeling sorry for himself and started counting his blessings, he thanked God for his "little chicken drumstick." The man can hold a pen and write like a pro with his little chicken drumstick. He is blessed! According to John Killinger, "Sometimes, because we are not thankful, we become sorry for ourselves, and feel neglected. . . . It is in being thankful that we see how truly rich we are."[6]

Bring Our Requests to God

Verse 6 in Philippians 4 says we should present our requests to God. That means *all* our requests! There's no problem too big for God. There's nothing so trivial that He does not care. When we stop obsessing over how big our problems are and start focusing on how big God is, peace flows forth in natural sequence.

I would love to tell you I haven't ever struggled with some of the issues in this chapter, but I can't. Honestly, I can't tell you the number of times I've prayed after I had relinquished my peace by worrying awhile. God is always faithful to answer prayers, even if we got there through a thatch of thorny of worries. During such situations when I hit the "replay" button in my mind, I usually recall the answer to prayer coming after I simply made my request to God. God knows our needs, but His word implores us to state our needs to Him. And it is so important to do exactly that if we want powerful answers.

When we rejoice, avoid worry, give thanks, and bring our requests to Him, we receive all God has for us. "The peace of God, which transcends all understanding, will guard your hearts and your minds in Christ Jesus" (Philippians 4:7). The word "guard" is a military term that implies soldiers guarding a priceless possession. Once this amazing peace is achieved, it guards our hearts and minds, but we should also guard our lives against anything that could snatch that peace from us.

On Guard

After presenting the general strategies for peace, Paul then admonishes us to guard our thought life in Philippians

4:8—"Finally, brothers, whatever is true, whatever is noble, whatever is right, whatever is pure, whatever is lovely, whatever is admirable—if anything is excellent or praiseworthy—think about such things." Sometimes this involves our willingness to fulfill another of Paul's admonishments found in 2 Corinthians 10:5, to "take captive every thought to make it obedient to Christ." Stormie Omartian states,

> Do certain negative thoughts play over and over in your mind? Do "what if" thoughts ever plague you? Or perhaps you dwell on "if only" regrets that cause you to question each decision you make. Do you ever think "No one cares about me." "Nothing ever turns out right for me." If you have had these thoughts, please know that this is not God giving you revelation for your life. These are words spoken to our souls by an enemy.
>
> We can overcome each of these lies with prayer, faith, and the truth of God's Word. When we fill our minds with God's Word and resources written by people in whom God's Spirit resides, and we listen to music that praises and glorifies Him, we leave no room for anything else.[7]

Understand that Satan would love to constantly destroy your peace. If he can't get at us through our circumstances or other people, then he will attack us with our own thought life. If he can't get into our thoughts directly, he'll do it subtly.

Advertisers have known for years just how powerful subliminal messages are. In a Canadian subliminal advertising blitz, a message was beamed at the rate of 600 times per minute. The message read, "Eat popcorn." The next day popcorn sales increased 85 per cent. So it goes with us. Whatever we dwell on will affect our actions and the directions of our lives. If we participate in negative conversations, dwell on what's wrong, and focus on our own shortcomings or those of others, then we are living a one-way ride to the land of no peace. If we read books that are filled with filth, watch movies that violate the Word of God, and listen to music that isn't pleasing to the Lord, then we are defeating the answers to our own prayers for inner tranquility. While God is the author of peace and will grant us that peace, we are also called to live spiritually responsible and embrace a thought life and lifestyle that breed peace.

> *There is a place of quiet rest,*
> *Near to the heart of God;*
> *A place where sin cannot molest,*
> *Near to the heart of God.*
>
> *There is a place of comfort sweet,*
> *Near to the heart of God;*
> *A place where we our Savior meet,*
> *Near to the heart of God.*
>
> *There is a place of full release,*
> *Near to the heart of God;*

A place where all is joy and peace,
Near to the heart of God.

O Jesus, blest Redeemer,
Sent from the heart of God,
Hold us, who wait before Thee,
Near to the heart of God.[8]

When Real Life Strikes

In his book *Then Sings My Soul*, Robert J. Morgan recounts the stories behind 150 of the world's greatest hymns. The song "Near to the Heart of God" is one of those songs. As with many masterpieces, there is a tragedy behind it. When Cleland B. McAfee wrote the song, he was serving as the pastor and director of the choir at Park University in Parkville, Missouri. Cleland's father, John A. McAfee, co-founded the college with Colonel George Park in 1875. All six of his adult children, including Cleland, served the college. After the song was published, Cleland's daughter, Katherine, told why her father wrote the hymn:

It was [my father's] custom, when communion services came, to write the words and music of a response which his choir could sing and which would fit into the theme of his sermon.

One terrible week, just before communion Sunday, the two little daughters of my Uncle Howard and Aunt

Lucy McAfee died of diphtheria within twenty-four hours of each other. The college family and town were stricken with grief. My father often told us how he sat long and late thinking of what could be said in word and song on the coming Sunday. . . .

So he wrote ["Near the to Heart of God"]. The choir learned it at the regular Saturday night rehearsal, and afterward they went to Howard McAfee's home and sang it as they stood under the sky outside the darkened, quarantined house. It was sung again on Sunday morning at the communion service.[9]

In the real world life sometimes throws us curves. Even the strongest Christian can become like Tiffany—unable to remember what peace tastes like. Loved ones tragically die. Financial losses happen. Difficult people can knock you flat. If you're in a bad situation that has destroyed your peace, don't despair. Don't beat yourself up and focus on your failures. Instead, sweep aside the things that are claiming your time and cluttering your life and fall to your knees. Re-connect with the Source of peace and do what His word says to reclaim your peace.

Second, do what God shows you on a specific level for your individual needs. What He shows you might not be easy, but He will give you the courage and strength to carry out what He deems your best interest. And remember throughout the process that "He who began a good work in you will carry it on to completion until the day of Christ Jesus" (Philippians 1:6).

> *What a Friend we have in Jesus,*
>   *All our sins and griefs to bear!*
> *What a privilege to carry*
>   *Everything to God in prayer!*
> *O what peace we often forfeit,*
>   *O what needless pain we bear,*
> *All because we do not carry*
>   *Everything to God in prayer!*[10]

7
The Right Attitude

❧

The effectual fervent prayer of a
rightcous man availeth much.
(*James 5:16, KJV*).

Our city is blessed with an old-fashioned train named the Texas State Railroad. It's owned by the same company that runs the famous train stretching from Silverton to Durango, Colorado. This past Christmas, the Texas State Railroad featured a fun ride based on the popular children's book *The Polar Express*. When we announced that our church was planning a group trip, the idea was met with great enthusiasm.

We were all excited the night of the train ride. After we boarded and the train began to roll, we sang carols and drank hot cocoa. My son had secured his first job on the train. He was one of the attendants—dressed as a chef. That made the trip even more special.

After we made it to the "North Pole" and were on our journey back to the train station, I needed to take a bathroom break. On my way to the restroom, I swayed with the rhythm of the train and chatted with people as I trudged up the aisle.

East Texas in December is usually weather schizophrenia. One day it's 20, and the next it's 65. One day it's sleeting, and the next there could be a tornado warning. We were fortunate that this night was in the 60s, so the windows were all open, which allowed a merry breeze to dance among my friends and cool my cheeks.

Once I introduced myself to the bathroom door, I realized I was going to need help bringing the old latch into submission. Finally, my son wrestled with the door long enough to get it open. That should have been my first clue, but I stepped inside and shut the door with no thought of the consequences. During my little visit, I reflected that the whole train looked as if it dated back to about 1850. Actually, the steam engines do indeed date back that far. Later I learned that the car I was in dated to the mid 1920s.

I assumed the brass door knob must have been original. Once it was time for me to exit, I was convinced it was. No matter how hard I tried, I could not get the knob to turn hard enough to open the door. I twisted and grunted and nearly spit, but the door remained closed.

The whole situation would have been bad enough if the bathroom were modern and had just been cleaned. But it was only one step removed from a construction workers' port-a-potty and did *not* smell like daisies.

After a final assault on the stubborn door knob, I decided to revert to another tactic: beating the walls. So I doubled my fists and pounded the metal walls in counter-rhythm to the train's clacking. The sounds of the train, a recording of *The Polar Express* playing over the speakers, and the noise of the crowd all drowned my attempts to draw attention to my predicament. Nevertheless, I pounded until my fists ached.

Finally, I looked at my watch and realized about ten minutes had lapsed and that there was only 15 minutes left in the ride. I thought, *I guess when I don't get off with the church group maybe they'll wonder what happened to me and come find me.*

I pounded some more. Then I decided to switch my tactics and pound the wall my friend Jennifer was sitting near. I beat that wall with a furor and screamed, "Jennifer! Jennifer!"

When that got me nowhere, I began to think this was a predicament you might read about in a Nancy Drew novel. And since I was trapped in there, maybe I should explore and see if I couldn't come up with a mystery. Of course, it took all of thirty seconds to look over every inch of the matchbox-sized restroom. The only hope I had for discovering any kind of a mystery lay behind a door under the sink, and it was bolted shut.

That's when I realized the panels along the outside wall were actually windows they had painted to prohibit anyone from looking into the restroom. On a surge of wild hope, I attempted to raise one of the windows. Expecting it to be wedged eternally in place, I was shocked when the window whisked up with one firm shove.

I leaned as close to the opening as I could get and screamed, "Jennifer! Jennifer!" Since the train's windows were open, I was confident that Jennifer would hear me. But I lost my grip on the window, and the thing slammed shut. Not one to accept defeat, I raised the window again and screamed for my friend as loudly as I could.

God hears no more than the heart

speaks; and if the heart be dumb,

God will certainly be deaf.

—Thomas Brooks

That's when I heard the door knob rattle. I turned around and bellowed, "Jennifer?"

"Debra, are you locked in?" she hollered.

"Yes!" I twisted the knob back and forth. Within a matter of seconds, she got my son once again to wrestle the latch open. The knob turned. The door opened. I was met with the laughter of friends and family. Welcoming the clean air, I stepped from "Nightmare in the Restroom" to freedom.

Trapped and Desperate

So many times my being locked in the restroom is very much like our prayer experience. We wait until we're in a stinky fix before we start pounding at heaven and asking for answers. Like a panicked passenger, we promise God we'll be missionaries in Botswana if he'll just get us out of this situation. We raise every window we can find and scream heavenward, "Help, God! Are you out there? I'm in a situation here! Can you hear me? *Please* get me out!"

In such predicaments, our faith in God's abilities soars in proportion to our panic. We desperately hope for answers to our prayers on a level we've not known in years. We even dare *expect* God to answer our prayers just as strongly as I expected my church family to come to my rescue. But, of course, we're "stuck," and getting answers to our prayers is our only way out. Therefore, the intensity is great! And in the midst of our despair, we hear ourselves repenting and promising God we'll do whatever He asks just as long as He pulls us through.

Then suddenly, one day we wake up and find our prayers are being answered! God *is* pulling us through. Everything we asked for is unfolding bit by bit, and we're rejoicing in His miraculous power. We testify in church to the Lord's hearing us when we call. Our faith is boosted. So is that of our friends and family.

But as the problem fades away and the crisis is over, too many believers go back to their old habits of not daily beseeching God for answers to prayer in every area of their lives. I am convinced that this type of existence is far removed from the best the Lord has for us and that He wants us to live a lifestyle of answered prayers. It's not His will for us to wait until we're trapped to begin to pound heaven's door. Even if everything is going well in our lives, He wants us to be so burdened for those around us that we bring their requests before His throne as well as our own.

The closer I walk with the Lord, the more convinced I am that many professing Christians have very little or no confidence in the power of prayer on a daily basis. They are blinded to the fact that the "prayer of a righteous man is powerful and effective" (James 5:16). Or perhaps they are so full of doubts that their answers are choked by their own lack of faith. Too many times believers can become like Huckleberry Finn when he says,

Miss Watson she took me in the closet and prayed, but nothing come of it. She told me to pray every day, and whatever I asked for I would get it. But it warn't so. I tried it. Once I got a fish-line, but no hooks. It warn't any good to me without hooks. I tried for the hooks three or four times, but somehow I couldn't make it work. By and by, one day, I asked Miss Watson to try for me, but she said I was a fool. She never told me why, and I couldn't make it out no way.

I set down one time back in the woods, and had a long think about it. I says to myself, if a body can get anything they pray for why don't Deacon Winn get back the money he lost on pork? Why can't the widow get back her silver snuff-box that was stole? Why can't Miss Watson fat up? No, says I to myself, there ain't nothing to it.[1]

There Really Is Something to It

If you're around the church about a week, you'll soon discover that we talk a lot about prayer, how important it is, the effects of prayer, and the answers to prayer. We are convinced that prayer is the definitive answer to all our problems. But for some, seeing any answers to prayers is within itself the problem. Like Huckleberry Finn, we can become so perplexed that we feel we need to seek guidance on how to pray, and sometimes those we seek guidance from are about as supportive as Miss Watson and act as if we're fools.

Of course, there are situations in life that are so mind-boggling that we really don't know how to pray. In those types of situations, we rely on the promise of Romans 8:26: "We do not know what we ought to pray for, but the Spirit himself intercedes for us." In these special cases we have no other recourse but to place it all in His hands.

But I'm talking about the everyday necessity for bringing our requests to God and living a lifestyle of answered prayers. I believe that perhaps one of the reason believers grow frustrated is because we are led to expect a great deal when we do pray. In Luke 11:9, Jesus himself says, "Ask and it will be given to you; seek and you will find; knock and the door will be opened to you." Therefore, when we do commit to asking on a daily basis and we don't see results, doubt is a natural outgrowth.

I don't propose to have all the answers to all problems. I know I haven't arrived spiritually. I'm still a work in progress, and every corner I turn in life affirms that God is a long way from finished with me. Nevertheless, I have managed to stumble into the kind of prayer life that reaps amazing results. We have a joke around our house. The kids often say something like "Don't get on Mom's bad side. She's liable to pray down lightning on your head, and God will zap you within the hour!" Of course, they're teasing. I would *never* pray for lightning to strike anyone. But I do pray for numerous requests daily, and I share the prayers and answers with my family. I especially want my kids to know that such an existence is possible for the one who commits to a holy life and walks in reverence of a holy God.

However, I didn't fall into this lifestyle of answered prayers overnight. It was a journey that took years for me to develop. And it all started with my willingness to follow Jesus' disciples when they asked Him to teach them to pray.

Teach Us to Pray

In her book *Each New Day,* Corrie ten Boom tells about a boy who needed help learning how to pray:

A mother saw her little boy sitting in a corner of the room, saying, "ABCDEFG."

"What are you doing?" she asked.

"Mom, you told me I should pray, but I have never prayed in my life and I don't know how. So I gave God the whole alphabet and asked Him to make a good prayer out of it."

That boy understood a little bit of what Paul says in Romans 8:26—that the Holy Spirit himself helps us to pray. Yes, He prays in us.[2]

In his book *Prayer: The Act of Being with God,* John Killinger wisely observes, "The problem is that people simply do not know *how* to pray."[3] The disciples were no exception.

When they began their journey with Christ, they were far from the spiritual giants they became before their deaths. Like all of us, they had major struggles, a lot of setbacks, and much to learn. One of the things they needed to learn was how to pray, so they asked Jesus to teach them.

Luke 11:1 states, "One day Jesus was praying in a certain place. When he finished, one of his disciples said to him, 'Lord, teach us to pray, just as John taught his disciples.'"

Understand that rabbis of their day always taught their disciples a prayer they could habitually use. John had been no exception. What Jesus' disciples were asking was quite the norm for their culture.

However, Jesus' disciples were following the Son of God. Therefore, His model prayer is by far the most powerful, meaningful, and effective of any that had gone before: "He said to them, 'When you pray, say: "Father, hallowed be your name, your kingdom come. Give us each day our daily bread. Forgive us our sins, for we also forgive everyone who sins against us. And lead us not into temptation"'" (Luke 11:2-4). Matthew 6:9-13 features the longer version of the Lord's Prayer that is most often recited.

Understand that the effectiveness of the rest of the prayer—or any of our prayers—rests within the first phrase, "Our Father in heaven, hallowed be your name." If we miss the importance of hallowing the name of our heavenly Father, we can forget the rest of the prayer. The word "hallowed" means, "May your name be held holy."

When we pray "Hallowed be your name," we are not requesting that God should become hallowed. God has been hallowed—the Holy One—from eternity to eternity. Rather, we're acknowledging God as the holy one and the God of holy love. We are revering God as the Almighty Creator, the Great I am, the Source of our very existence.

Isaiah 6:1-3 testifies to this truth: "I saw the Lord seated on a throne, high and exalted, and the train of his robe filled the temple. Above him were seraphs, each with six wings: With two wings they covered their faces, with two they covered their feet, and with two they were flying. And they were calling to one another: 'Holy, holy, holy is the LORD Almighty; the whole earth is full of his glory.'" Revelation 4:8 details the four living creatures around the throne of God: "Day and night they never stop saying: 'Holy, holy, holy is the Lord God Almighty, who was, and is, and is to come.'"

When we know God is holy, we stand in awe of and revere Him just as the four living creatures do. But before we can truly revere Him, we have to fully embrace the fact that He is a holy God, that He is perfectly pure, void of evil, full of love.

If we want powerful answers to our prayers, it all starts with getting our attitudes right toward God. If we view God as some sort of heavenly Santa Claus who exists for the sole purpose of delivering us when we're trapped or filling our list of desired items like some grocery boy, then we'll be in the same boat with Huckleberry Finn. Rather, if we hold an indescribable awe for the Holy God, Creator of all, then it changes the very fabric of our requests. They flow out of an intimate relationship with God from a heart that is beating in sequence with His.

When this depth of relationship occurs, then an awe of God fills our being, and we want to show Him that we believe He is hallowed in every area of our lives. So, of course, we tell Him. But God also wants us to *show* Him daily. This can happen no better way than our fulfilling 1 Peter 1:15-16: "Just as he who called you is holy, so be holy in all you do; for it is written: 'Be holy, because I am holy.'" The wonderful thing about God is that He doesn't ask us to do something He isn't eager to do in us and through us. In our human power, none of us can even come close to being holy. But God can make us holy through His power. All He asks is that we revere Him enough to give Him first place in our hearts.

When He holds first place in our hearts, we live a lifestyle that shows Him reverence. This means we are constantly aware of Him and never forget Him in anything we do. When we refuse to live a lifestyle of reverencing Him, we cut ourselves off from the eternal source of love and the One who moves and answers our prayers. Just showing up at church on Sunday morning is not a free ticket to having our prayers answered. *Anyone* can go to church on Sunday morning.

My husband's friend Clyde Jenkins is an usher in a megachurch in Houston. In large churches, the ushers could sometimes be better described as bouncers. He has some wild stories about encounters with unusual people. One of those people arrived one Sunday morning looking more like Satan than not. He had trained his goatee to come to a well-groomed point. He also had a pair of horns implanted in his scalp. Clyde says he told him he was welcome but that he didn't want any trouble.

The man said, "Okay." So he sat in the service awhile and then finally got up and left while mumbling, "I don't need to be here."

Even though that man attended church that Sunday morning, I have serious doubts about his intimacy with God or his propensity toward living a lifestyle of answered prayers. Anybody who tries to make himself or herself look like the devil is serving the wrong master. Whether a person actually looks like the devil or not, if he or she is serving the wrong master, then the person can't expect to have phenomenal answers to prayer—even if he or she is in church regularly. Amazing answers to prayer happen only for those who are immersed in the presence of God and determine to follow His will every day.

James 5:16 states, "The effectual fervent prayer of a *righteous* man availeth much" (KJV). Throughout this book, I talked about God's call to live a life of righteousness, free of willful, known sin. Sometimes God's moving in the face of our requests is in direct proportion to our willingness to relinquish our pet sins. According to Evelyn Christenson,

> The prophet Isaiah gives a powerful description of someone in this plight: "Listen now! The Lord isn't too weak to save you. And he isn't getting deaf! He can hear you when you call! But the trouble is that your sins have cut you off from God. Because of sin He has turned His face away from you and will not listen anymore" (Isaiah 59:1-2, TLB).
>
> Do you wonder why your prayers aren't answered? Here is the first [reason]: sin (or sins) in your life. It is "the effectual, fervent prayer of a *righteous* person that availeth much." If your prayers aren't availing much, this may be the reason. Maybe it isn't. Maybe you're long past this. But I find that when I think I'm past this one, all at once a little pride pops up, and I have to confess it quickly, get it out, and then go on.[4]

Committing to a deep relationship with God means we're committing to turn our backs on pride and self-righteousness. These are areas where so many miss the mark, and when God shows us that we are missing the mark, we are called to confess it as if it were a willful, known sin. Because at the point that God make us aware of a certain area we are blind to, it ceases to be missing the mark and will become willful, known sin if we do not confess and repent. According to Corrie ten Boom, "The blood of Jesus does not cleanse excuses. It cleanses sins that are confessed. We have to humble ourselves."[5]

Such a lifestyle leads to continual communion with the Lord. Therefore, when we do present our requests to Him, we are asking from the outpouring of a vital and close relationship with Him—a relationship not marred by our prideful unwillingness to confess where we have failed. People who regularly get powerful answers to prayer are the ones who steadfastly seek Him, hallow His name, confess and repent as He reveals the need, and relinquish all to Him *as a lifestyle,* in the good times and the bad. In Luke and Matthew both, the prayer Christ gave to His disciples starts with hallowing God's holy name, then moves to His will being done, and finally deals with presenting our needs to Him.

Your Will Be Done

I have encountered numerous written and verbal stories about a patient who is near death and a praying mother or father who is begging God to allow their child to live. Amazingly, the story is always the same. The parent is in the hospital room or bedroom of the dying child. He or she is begging God to let the child live and offering everything, even his or her own life, as an exchange for God to miraculously move.

Finally, after hours of struggling and trying to convince God to touch the child, the parent wilts and weeps and somehow squeaks out a relinquishment to God's perfect will, "O Lord, if it's your will for this child to die, then take her [him] to be with you. You know what the future holds. I accept what you want for her [his] life and mine."

At that point, an amazing thing always happens. The sick child stirs in bed. The parent goes to check the fever to find that it has diminished or disappeared. The child begins to miraculously improve and is soon well again.

One of the things I have learned is that God works in patterns. When I hear a similar story related from different people in different parts of the world in different time eras, I usually pay close attention to the pattern, because there is much to be learned about the way God works through the generations by observing these patterns.

In her book *Adventures in Prayer*, Catherine Marshall writes about the "Law of Relinquishment." This law is what I believe is manifested in these repeated stories. When we stop trying to manipulate God with our requests and stop praying our answers, then—and only then—does God move according to His divine will. According to Evelyn Christenson, "When we pray for answers, we're demanding that God do something and telling Him we want it done now—'just the way we want it, Lord.' When we're bringing our requests to Him, we're saying, 'Lord, here's the need' (the circumstance, the person, whatever it may be); then we ask Him to answer according to His omniscient will."[6] That is not to say we shouldn't be specific in what we pray for. The next chapter deals with asking God for specifics and being persistent. However, even in persistently asking for specifics, our spirit should be meekly bowed before a holy God and conforming to His will for the given situation—not pounding Him for what *we* want with little thought for His divine plan.

Many times fear drives us to desperately pound at God for the answers we demand. We're terrified of losing our child, mate, job, finances, home, and way of life. The fear so spiritually paralyzes us that we lose sight of God as the ever-loving Father who is ultimately in control of our lives and wants the best for us.

According to Catherine Marshall,

We are squarely up against the Law of Relinquishment. Was Jesus showing us how to use this law when He said, "Resist not evil"? Stop fleeing from and denying this terrible prospect. Look squarely at the possibility of what you fear most. . . . So we take the first hard steps of obedience. And lo, as we stop hiding our eyes, force ourselves to walk up to the fear and look it full in the face—never forgetting that God and His power are still the supreme reality—the fear evaporates. Drastic? Yes. But it is one sure way of releasing prayer power into human affairs.[7]

None of this is to say that *everything* that happens in life is God's perfect will. Viewing life and God in this vein makes God the author of sin. For instance, I've seen situations such as that of the three-year-old who was brutally raped, murdered, and thrown into a ditch; and Christians are angry at God because they've been taught to believe that absolutely everything that happens is His divine will. No! It's never His will for children to be victimized. That is clearly the work of Satan.

God gives people a *choice* to obey Him or follow Satan and live in sin. When they choose sin, then it can and does detrimentally impact others. Given this truth, we have to use balance and common sense in embracing the Law of Relinquishment. In this story of the victimized three-year-old, her parents allowed her to play with her siblings, unattended, at a deserted parking lot near their home.

The Law of Relinquishment does not mean that we relinquish all sensible responsibility or view every evil act as God's perfect will. It does mean that we do everything humanly possible and then humbly leave the outcome in God's hands. As already alluded to in chapter three, the Law of Relinquishment is ultimately about releasing control to God and His wisdom to do what is best in any given situation, rather than telling God what is best in our eyes. And that's what it means to say, "Your will be done."

According to Evelyn Christenson,

And there we see the beginning of prayer: the becoming attuned or connected with God, the Source of all strength and power. No need to turn on the switch, seeking the blessings of prayer, until first our lives become properly connected to God. This is why so many fail to get what they ask in prayer.

—Charles L. Allen[9]

The Lord's prayer really comes into focus right where we are when we pray, "Thy will be done on earth as it is in heaven." Is there anything contrary to God's will in heaven? No! Think of what would happen if every Christian really brought God's will to the little sphere that is his, with nothing contrary to God's perfect will! How different would be our nation, our cities, our churches, our homes.[8]

8

The Answers

❧

Ask and it will be given to you; seek
and you will find; knock and the
door will be opened to you.
For everyone who asks receives;
he who seeks finds; and to him who
knocks, the door will be opened
(Luke 11:9-10).

As already mentioned in chapter four, we own five cats. Two of them are outside cats, and three of them can't decide whether they want to live inside or out. Of course, since we are their loyal servants, our sole purpose in life is to be ready to open the door whenever they decide they want a change of scenery. That usually happens immediately following breakfast—which they expect the second I get up.

Every morning when I slide out of bed, one or two of my cats are sitting somewhere in my bedroom. They stare at me as if they are trying to put me in some sort of a cat-feeding trance. I call this "stage one harassment." Sometimes one of them is perched on the end of the bed or hovering near the doorway. Therefore, the first living creature I see every morning is one of those cats. And they always have an agenda: *breakfast!* It's the only time of the day they get canned food, and it is indeed a sacred moment for them. To miss it is to *die!* At least you would think that by the way they howl.

The howling usually starts after they grant me permission to make a stop in the restroom. Once I exit that chamber, they get serious about pestering me into feeding them. All stage one antics are over. We are now to stage two: vocal stalking. By this point, they are rubbing against me and meowing as if they haven't eaten in *weeks.*

And heaven help the person who tries to ignore them. They get so loud and persistent that you would be willing to tape their mouths shut if you could. I remember one Saturday morning when my husband got up before I did. I meandered down to the kitchen and noticed that the cats were unusually quiet. I asked Daniel if he'd already fed them, and he said, "Yes! I had to! They harassed me!" All I know is, if they can sway a grown man the size of a linebacker who doesn't even *want* cats, they have some persuasive tenacity that borders on miraculous.

But when they're dealing with me, I would feed them whether they harassed me or not—because I love my cats. I've always loved cats and have had cats since my earliest childhood memories. When I was in junior high school, I remember one of my cats being run over by a car. I cried the way I would if my sister had died. I always tell non-cat-lovers that when they get right with Jesus, they'll love cats as much as I do. My husband has even asked me a time or two if he should be jealous of Tiger, my sweet, striped tabby; but I have assured Daniel that he still holds first place in my heart.

Since I love my cats so much, I want what's best for them. I know they need their breakfast before they even ask. And I would willingly dish it out for them whether they harass me or not. They've all been with me nine to ten years—since they were babies—and I'm committed to caring for them until they die.

If a mere mortal can commit to caring for and meeting the needs of her cats to this level, then how much more does

God care for those whom He has created? If He loved us so much that He stretched himself out on the Cross for our sins, then we can be assured He loves us enough to hear and answer our prayers. He really does want what's best for us. We can be confident that no matter what life throws at us, He is there to hear us, deliver us, and direct us.

Our job is to place enough faith in Him to consecrate ourselves to serious prayer. According to Catherine Marshall,

> In order to make sure that we are not retreating from the tension of faith, it is helpful to ask ourselves as we pray, *Do I really expect anything to happen?* This will prevent us from going window-shopping in prayer. At times window-shopping can be enjoyable—but there it ends. It costs nothing. We are just looking, have no intention of buying anything; so we bring nothing home to show for the hours of browsing. Too many of our prayers—private and public—are just browsing amongst possible petitions, not down to cases at all. We expect nothing from our prayers except perhaps a euphoric feeling.[1]

There are several steps to a prayer life that reaps consistent answers from God rather than a mere euphoric feeling. As already mentioned, the first step is to allow God to impart His holiness to us by placing Him on the throne of our hearts and consecrating ourselves to a righteous life. According to Charles L. Allen,

With God all things are possible.

—Matthew 19:26

In the fourth chapter of the Epistle of James, we read these words: "Ye ask, and receive not, because ye ask amiss." In the same chapter James tells us: "Submit yourselves therefore to God." On further he says, "Draw nigh to God, and he will draw nigh to you." Also, James says, "Humble yourselves in the sight of the Lord, and he shall lift you up." The beginning of prayer is a right relationship with God; without that beginning we merely speak words and call them prayers.[2]

The second step is to hallow His name to the point that we never enter into prayer flippantly but rather, in a state of awe of who He is. The third step is to make certain our hearts are wholly submitted to His will. And the final step is very simple: persistently ask Him.

Persistent Prayer

After Jesus' disciples asked him to teach them to pray, He didn't stop with just the Lord's Prayer. In Luke 11:5-13 He went on to relate a truth about prayer that encouraged the disciples (and us) that they, too, could get results:

He said unto them, Which of you shall have a friend, and shall go unto him at midnight, and say unto him, Friend, lend me three loaves; For a friend of mine in his journey is come to me, and I have nothing to set before him? And he from within shall answer and say, Trouble me not: the door is now shut, and my children are with me in bed; I cannot rise and give thee. I say unto you, Though he will not rise and give him, because he is his friend, yet because of his importunity he will rise and give him as many as he needeth. And I say unto you, Ask, and it shall be given you; seek, and ye shall find; knock, and it shall be opened unto you. For every one that asketh receiveth; and he that seeketh findeth; and to him that knocketh it shall be opened. If a son shall ask bread of any of you that is a father, will he give him a stone? or if he ask a fish, will he for a fish give him a serpent? Or if he shall ask an egg, will he offer him a scorpion?

If ye then, being evil, know how to give good gifts unto your children: how much more shall your heavenly Father give the Holy Spirit to them that ask him? (KJV).

To fully understand this passage, it's important to know the social issues that surround the setting. Travelers in Jesus' day usually rested in the heat of the day and traveled late in the evening, when it was cool. They didn't have hotel chains on every corner and often stayed with friends. When this traveler stopped at his friend's house, he had no telephone or e-mail to notify his friend ahead of time that he was coming. He was a surprise visitor, and the friend was not ready for him. Since the friend couldn't run to the grocery deli as we would, he went to his neighbor's place to ask for bread.

However, the door was shut. In their culture, a shut door was the same as a "Do Not Disturb" sign in today's world.

Now, during the day the door would have been wide open so the kids and chickens could roam freely. There was very little privacy in the daytime. But at night, if the door was shut, it was a serious cultural violation for someone to disturb the family inside.

Nevertheless, the man knocked anyway. This was considered the height of rudeness. But the man had a duty to his friend that drove him to ignore social etiquette. In the East, not having something to give a traveling friend was not just an embarrassment—it was a violation of a sacred duty. Not only was the guest to be provided a meal, but it was the custom to give him more than enough. Since families baked only enough bread for each day, it was common for the host to be out of bread. Because the friend couldn't fulfill his sacred duty, he resorted to his only option. He went to his neighbor's home and pounded the door. His obligation to provide a meal for the visitor superseded his respect for the neighbor's closed door.

Not only did he pound the door, but he also told the neighbor what he wanted as he pounded: "Friend, loan me three loaves of bread, because a friend of mine on a journey has come to me, and I have nothing to set before him." The reason he asked for three loaves was significant. The guest would have one. Since it was considered an insult to let the guest eat alone, the host would eat one with his friend. And the third loaf would be left uneaten to provide evidence of plenty of food. Therefore, the guest would not be embarrassed into thinking he had eaten all the host's food.

So the man continues to knock on the neighbor's door and finally wakes him up. The neighbor is *not* a happy camper! He's as irritated as any of us would be if someone were pounding on our door in the middle of the night, demanding three loaves of bread. The man next door doesn't care that the traveler has nothing to eat. He just wants some sleep! Even though he understands his neighbor's sacred duty to provide a meal for the guest, he also feels the pain of someone seriously overstepping social mores and ignoring the fact that his door is shut.

So the guy says something like "Get lost! Stop bothering me! The door is shut and locked, for crying out loud. The whole family is in bed! I absolutely will not get up to give you a thing!"

In our eyes, it might seem simple for the man just to get up, grab three loaves, open the door, hurl them at the man, slam the door, and then flop back into bed. But that was not their reality. The house next door was very likely typical of most houses in that era. Most were one-room with a single, small window. Dried grass blanketed the dirt floor. A raised platform took up one-third of the floor. That's where the stove burned all night. Rather than sleeping on raised beds, the family slept on mats. They didn't each have a room of their own. Instead, they all slept together around the stove in order to stay warm.

Now, imagine the man getting up. He would disturb his wife and all his children—who won't necessarily go back to sleep easily. On top of all that, the livestock also slept in the house at night: chickens, goats, sheep, a dog, maybe even a cat or two. No wonder the neighbor is exasperated! There was absolutely no graceful, silent way to answer the door without a major upheaval of the wife, the kids, and the cackling chickens, not to mention a disturbed goat or two.

The man at the door fully understands everything the neighbor has to go through to give him the loaves. Nevertheless, he brazenly knocks despite the neighbor's exasperation. At long last, the neighbor sees that the man is not going to stop until he gives him the bread. Only because of the man's tenacity does the neighbor go through the whole rigmarole of waking the family and livestock to give him what he wants. In Luke 11:8 Jesus said, "I tell you, though he will not get up and give him the bread because he is his friend, yet because of the man's boldness he will get up and give him as much as he needs."

Luke 18 relates a different parable with the same theme: "In a certain town there was a judge who neither feared God nor cared about men. And there was a widow in that town who kept coming to him with the plea 'Grant me justice against my adversary'" (vv. 1-3). Understand that judges were exceedingly corrupt. The person with the most money was often the one who won the case. This poor widow had no bribe money, so the judge gave her no consideration. Nevertheless, the widow refused to stop. She kept on keeping on and pestered the man half to death. (Sounds a lot like my cats in the morning!) Finally, he said, "Even though I don't fear God or care about men, yet because this widow keeps bothering me, I will see that she gets justice, so that she won't eventually wear me out with her coming!'" (vv. 4-5).

Both of these parables have the same message. A grouchy, sleepy neighbor and a crooked judge are contrasted with God. The neighbor had no desire to give his friend bread, and the evil judge had no plans to give the widow justice. Jesus' conclusion of the parable about the widow and judge aptly fits both parables."Listen to what the unjust judge says. And will not God bring about justice for his chosen ones, who cry out to him day and night? Will he keep putting them off? I tell you, he will see that they get justice, and quickly" (Luke 18:6-8). In other words, God is so much more willing and ready to answer his children's prayers than a crooked judge or a sleepy neighbor; all we have to do is ask. These parables emphasize two important truths about God's answering prayers: He is approachable and He is eager and willing to hear from us.

Jesus underscores His point in verse 9: "So I say to you: Ask and it will be given to you; seek and you will find; knock and the door will be opened to you." This means to repeatedly ask and you will receive, perpetually seek and you will find, and continually knock and it will be opened to you. The widow was tenacious in her asking. The neighbor refused to give up knocking. Since God is ready to listen to us and answer our prayers, we should be heartened to never give up in our quest to ask, seek, and knock.

In Luke 11:11, Jesus further states that even mortal dads provide the needs of their children. In their culture, there was a stone that was the exact shape and color of a loaf of bread. Jesus' point was that a caring father wouldn't mock the child's needs by giving him such a stone. Furthermore, if a son asked for a fish, a loving father wouldn't give him a serpent. Some scholars believe that Jesus actually referenced an eel, which was unclean for the Jewish diet. In other words, a father wouldn't give his son something detrimental to his health or religious beliefs. As for the scorpion, there was a small, cream-colored scorpion that resembled an egg when he tucked his legs and tail beneath him. No decent father would give his child a scorpion that could hurt him instead of an egg that would bring nourishment. Jesus said, "If you then, though you are evil, know how to give good gifts to your children, how much more will your Father in heaven give the Holy Spirit to those who ask him!" (Luke 11:13).

Jesus was encouraging us to never give up, to continually ask, seek, and knock. We are called to relinquish the outcome and control to God and let Him answer in His time and way. However, understand that He *wants* to answer our prayers and supply our needs according to what is best for us. That doesn't mean we will get everything we ask for; but it does mean we can be assured that God will not mock our prayers. Sometimes we don't know the future, and the things we ask for will be detrimental to us if God were to grant them. We must accept that God is all-seeing and all-knowing and that He answers according to His wisdom. Notice in Luke 11:13 that Jesus ends this passage by saying that God will give the Holy Spirit to anyone who asks. When we pray for the fullness of the Spirit, every believer can be assured he or she is praying in God's will. And in all things we are called to "Devote yourselves to prayer, being watchful and thankful" (Colossians 4:2).

According to Catherine Marshall,

> After watching a procession of [miracles], gradually the disciples came to know this as Jesus' way. "Tell Me exactly what you want," He was always saying. "Talk to me. *Ask* me."

> The importance of expressing our needs to our heavenly Father was a point He came back to over and over in His teaching: how much more will your Father in heaven give good gifts to those who *ask* him?

> *Ask* and the gift will be yours, for everyone who asks receives. *Ask* and you will receive, that your joy may be full.[3]

Somebody said to me: "When I worry I go to the mirror and say to myself, 'This tremendous thing which is worrying me is beyond solution. It is especially too hard for Jesus Christ to handle.' After I have said that, I smile and I am ashamed." "Do not be anxious about anything, but in everything, by prayer and petition, with thanksgiving, present your requests to God"

(Philippians 4:6-7).

—Corrie ten Boom[5]

Perhaps the reason Jesus emphasized that we should keep on asking was so we would develop a prayer habit—not an on-again, off-again routine but a lifelong habit. Catherine Marshall further states,

God insists that we ask, not because *He* needs to know our situation, but because *we* need the spiritual discipline of asking. Similarly, making our requests specific forces us to take a step forward in faith. The reason many of us retreat into vague generalities when we pray is not because we think too highly of God, but because we think too little. If we pray for something definite and our request is not granted, we fear to lose the little faith we had. So we fall back on the safe route of highly "spiritual" prayers— the kind that Jesus brushed aside as not true prayer at all, just self-deceptive "talking to ourselves."[4]

Definite Action

When we talk about answers to prayer, God has shown me that there are two basic categories of answers. There are the answers that He and He alone can answer, like the child dying and the physicians have done all they can do. Only *He* can step in and miraculously heal that child. This type of answer is the *miracle answer*. Sometimes the miracles are huge—like the airplane that amazingly avoids crashing into the side of the mountain. Sometimes the miracles are small-er—like the check that comes the very day the electric bill is due. Whether great or small, these miraculous answers are always grounds for shouting!

The other type of answers is what I call *Practical Answers*. These answers come in the form of something God often shows us we should do to bring about the answer we are seeking. Granted, the only way we can know what we need to do is by being still before Him and listening for His direction. Then we must have the courage to do exactly what He shows us. I have found that, especially regarding the issue of relationships, He knows what needs to happen in order to bring about the needed changes. It's my job to do what He shows me.

Over a decade ago, my good friend Frances Shaw was having trouble with her word processing program. We were talking on the phone, and I told her that I would help her get through the issue one step at a time if she would just press the buttons I told her to press in the sequence I instructed. She agreed.

One at a time, I told her what measures to take. Her phone was not wireless. When I told her what buttons to push, she would lay down the phone, go to the computer, and do exactly what I told her to do. Then she would come back to the phone, tell me the results, and we would move on to the next step. At the end of about ten minutes, she had pressed a series of buttons that had corrected her problem and set her up to begin word processing once more. She was so thankful and relieved.

The process worked beautifully, but only because she co-operated. If she had argued with me or pressed buttons other than the ones I told her to, she wouldn't have had positive results. Her problem would not have been solved. Neither would it have been solved if she had just sat down and re-fused to do anything I told her.

This situation is an excellent example of how God uses the practical method of answering prayers. Sometimes when we lift our requests to Him, He instructs us what to do to bring about the results we are seeking. Our job is to sit with Him long enough to determine if He requires our action in the answering process.

But too many times we lump every answer to prayers in the miracle category. We want to tell God our requests and then sit down in our easy chair and expect Him to just zap the whole situation to our specifications. According to Cor-rie ten Boom, "Prayer should never be an excuse for inaction. Nehemiah prayed, but he also set watches for protection—he used common sense. As a result, what had not been done in a hundred years' time was finished in fifty-two days. 'So the wall was finished . . in fifty-two days' (Nehemiah 6:15 RSV)."[6]

Consider all the situations in the Old Testament where God required people to do something before He brought about the answer to a prayer. When Moses and the children of Israel faced the Red Sea on one side and the Egyptian army on the other, God told Moses to raise his staff and stretch out his hand over the sea; only then did God part it (Exodus 14). When the children of Israel needed to defeat Jericho, God commanded them first to march around the city (Joshua 6). The walls collapsed after they obeyed. These are just two examples of very practical things God told people to do in order to bring about answers to prayer.

Like the walls of Jericho, so many bad situations in our lives can be crumbled to non-existence if we'll just take the time to listen to God and do *exactly* what He says. Sometimes it might not make sense in our human understanding. How much sense does it make to walk around stone walls and expect them to collapse? None! Not in human logic, anyway. But God is all-seeing and all-knowing. He knows exactly what measures it takes to alter situations and bring about the answers to prayers—no matter how desperate we are.

According to Catherine Marshall, "My most spectacular answers to prayers have come when I was so helpless, so out of control as to be able to do nothing at all for myself."[7]

None of this is to undermine our dire need for God's miraculous intervention as well as His practical guidance. Even when there is something we need to do to catapult a situation into a divine answer, we still must tune into the source of all wisdom and do what He says and *only* what He says. Sometimes that involves things we must *begin* doing;

other times it involves things we must *stop* doing—or never even start. According to John Killinger,

> Paul Tournier, the Swiss physician, said that one of the most important aspects of his prayer has always been to have God tell him what he should *not* undertake to do. Praying in that way has helped him keep his schedule simpler and more manageable and has doubtless prolonged his life, for there are many calls upon his time.
>
> David prayed about the Temple he wanted to build for God, said Dr. Tournier, and God told him not to build it. If David had disregarded that and built the Temple, it would have been a sin, even though David would have been doing it for God.
>
> "In the same way today, God will tell us not to do certain things that in themselves seem very praiseworthy."[8]

Many times there are more things for me to do in a day than there are hours to do it. For instance, as I was trying to finish writing this book, we wound up moving. Many days I would ask God, "Show me how to line up my day. Show me what to do first and how to manage everything I need to do." His practical guidance of what I should and should not do kept me from pulling my hair out with what could have been an over-the-top stressful situation. I rested in Him as I did the best I could. His unfathomable grace and practical guidance were the answers to my daily prayers.

According to Corrie ten Boom, "When a house is on fire and you know that there are people in it, it is a sin to straighten pictures in that house. When the world about you is in great danger, works that are in themselves not sinful can be quite wrong."[9] Many times the answers to our prayers lie in wholly aligning ourselves with the agenda of God and doing only what He shows us to do while weeding all excessive doing from our lives. This practical task alone can bring answers to prayer regarding our health, our marriages, our peace and tranquility, and our relationship with our children.

For example, many wonderful Christian people have children who have strayed from the faith and from their families. Many prayer meetings around the country will involve requests for these prodigals. Many times, but not always, there's an underlying problem with the whole family. The answer to the problem can be found in that parent developing a habit of being still before God, tuning into Him, and listening for the practical steps that he or she must take in order to bring about that child's redemption. Sometimes it might involve tough love and drawing hard boundaries. Other times it might involve getting into the child's space and showing him or her up-close, unconditional love. Or maybe it involves a plan only God himself knows. But until we stop doing all the unnecessary things in our lives and create time to listen to God and absorb His practical guidance, we never see the answers to such prayers.

Sometimes in life every one of

us finds himself out of control,

caught in circumstances that he

is helpless to change. When this

happens, welcome such times!

Often it is only then that we

lesser spirits enter into the truth

of Jesus' statement from the

fifteenth chapter of John:

"Apart from Me ye

can do nothing."

—Catherine Marshall[10]

Whatever the case, whether a prodigal child or a financial crisis, each situation is different and will require a different answer. It's up to us to develop a divine romance with God. In the midst of that romance, He will tell us whether we should do nothing and wait on His miracle or take the practical measures He reveals.

APPENDIX
Occultist or Satanic Items

Secular hard rock music. Many secular rock groups dedicate their albums to Satan.

Any posters, albums, cassette discs or clothing that feature hard rock groups or symbols.

Occult jewelry and staffs, which include

Egyptian ankh: a cross with a loop at the top.

Peace symbol

Italian good luck horn

Fairy wand

Leprechaun's staff

The evil eye: a hand with the index and little finger pointing up.

Polynesian tikis: carved to represent various gods.

Things such as **clovers, stars, wishbones, lucky coins, mystic medals**, and **mystic crystals**. Some beautiful works of art are carved in crystal; some keepsake glassware is made of crystal. These types of keepsakes are not the crystals that are dedicated to the New Age religious practices.

Pictures of anything demonic or cultic.

Zodiac signs, horoscopes, traditional symbols of Halloween.

New Age symbols.

Evil and violent-looking toys and figures.

R-rated and X-rated movies that you attend or get through subscription television, rental videos, or the Internet.

Ouija boards

Games such as Dungeons and Dragons

All forms of pornography: graphic photos or videos featuring nudity, or novels that depict descriptive sex scenes. Many women are as addicted to these types of novels as are some men who are addicted to Internet porn.

* * *

Remember to keep a sensible approach in these matters. Furthermore, when dealing with children, always try to replace something you take away. For instance, we carve smiley faces and crosses into pumpkins in the fall, rather than demonic faces. We don't totally throw out carving pumpkins, because it's something my kids enjoy. I allow my kids to dress up in non-scary or biblical costumes at our church's Fall Fest, which replaces Halloween.

Not reading or subscribing to the whole newspaper because it contains the horoscope is unbalanced. On the other hand, reading your horoscope daily and making decisions based on it does not reflect a life of faith in Christ.

Remember: clovers, stars, and the like aren't evil within themselves; it's the way they are presented. Using a clover or star as a good-luck symbol is not in line with trusting God. A painting of a wizard surrounded by stars would be something to avoid. A photo or painting of a beautiful, starry night would be acceptable. In other words, don't have knee-jerk reactions such as throwing out the star that goes on top of your Christmas tree or hyperventilating over a star charm on a bracelet.

Make decisions with God's guidance and wisdom. Chances are high that if you're already in tune with the Lord, you'll need to make very few or no adjustments.

NOTES

Chapter One

1. Sandra D. Wilson, *Into Abba's Arms: Finding the Acceptance You've Always Wanted* (Wheaton, Ill.: Tyndale House Publishers, 1998), 33.

2. Oswald Chambers, *My Utmost for His Highest* (Leicester, England: Ulverscroft, 1927), 43.

3. From *Knowing God,* by J. I. Packer, as quoted in Bob and Michael Benson's *Disciplines for the Inner Life* (Nashville: Word, 1985), 77.

4. William W. Walford, "Sweet Hour of Prayer," *Worship in Song* (Kansas City: Lillenas Publishing Company, 1972), 475.

5. Charles L. Allen, *All Things Are Possible Through Prayer* (Carmel, N.Y.: Guideposts, 1958), 3.

6. C. S. Lewis, "First and Second Things," in *Readings for Meditation and Reflection*, ed. Walter Hooper (San Francisco: HarperCollins, 1992), 14.

7. Stormie Omartian, *The Power of Praying: Help for a Woman's Journey Through Life* (Eugene, Oreg.: Harvest House, 2004), 87

8. David A. Seamands, *Putting Away Childish Things,* quoted in *Healing Your Heart of Painful Memories* (Edison, N.J.: Inspirational Press, 1993), 227

9. Chambers, *My Utmost for His Highest*, 39.

10. Omartian, *The Power of Praying,* 56

11. Corrie ten Boom, *Each New Day* (Boston: G. K. Hall & Co., 1978), 124-25.

Chapter Two

1. Michael Phillips, *Make Me Like Jesus: The Courage to Pray Dangerously* (Colorado Springs: Waterbrook, 2003), 3

2. Chambers, *My Utmost for His Highest*, 83.

3. Ibid., 114.

4. Omartian, *The Power of Praying,* 91.

5. Wilson, *Into Abba's Arms*, 32.

6. ten Boom, *Each New Day*, 174.

7. John Killinger, *Prayer: The Act of Being with God* (Waco, Tex.: Word, 1981), 11.

8. Claire Cloninger, *101 Most Powerful Prayers in the Bible*, Steve and Lois Rabey, gen. eds. (New York: Warner, 2003), 3.

Chapter Three

1. Paul S. Taylor, <http://www.christiananswers.net/q-eden /edn-t018.html>.

2. Catherine Marshall, *Adventures in Prayer* (Old Tappan, N.J.: Chosen, 1975), 52-53.

3. Omartian, *The Power of Praying*, 36.

4. Marshall, *Adventures in Prayer*, 53.

5. Ibid., 26.

6. Omartian, *The Power of Praying*, 54.

7. Adam Clarke, *Adam Clarke's Commentary on the Bible*, abridged by Ralph Earle (Kansas City: Beacon Hill Press of Kansas City, 1967), 282.

8. Ibid., 283.

9. Omartian, *The Power of Praying*, 72.

10. Larry Burnett, testimony received via e-mail. Used by permission.

Chapter Four

1. ten Boom, *Each New Day*, 27.

2. Omartian, *The Power of Praying*, 94.

3. Bruce Wilkinson, *The Prayer of Jabez: Breaking Through to the Blessed Life* (Sisters, Oreg.: Multnomah, 2000), 67.

4. Evelyn Christenson, assisted by Viloa Blake, *What Happens When Women Pray*, quoted in *Changing Your Life Through the Power of Prayer* (New York: Inspirational Press, 1993), 16.

5. Ibid., 19.

Chapter Five

1. Shirley Porter, personal testimony. Used by permission.

2. Ibid.

3. Chambers, *My Utmost for His Highest*, 12.

4. Omartian, *The Power of Praying*, 66.
5. Haldor Lillenas, "Glorious Freedom," *Sing to the Lord* (Kansas City: Lillenas Publishing Co., 1993), 505.
6. Omartian, *The Power of Praying*, 56.
7. Lillenas, "Glorious Freedom." 505.
8. Ibid.
9. Killinger, *Prayer: The Act of Being with God*, 60, 62-63.
10. Charles L. Allen, *All Things Are Possible Through Prayer* (Carmel, NY: Guideposts, 1958). 11.
11. Corrie ten Boom, *Each New Day* (Boston: G.K. Hall & Co., 1978). 56.
12. Sabine Baring-Gould, "Onward, Christian Soldiers," *Sing to the Lord* (Kansas City: Lillenas Publishing Co., 1993), 644.

Chapter Six

1. Allen, *All Things Are Possible Through Prayer*, 29.
2. Ibid., 67.
3. Ibid., 91
4. Ibid., 30.
5. Johnson Oatman Jr., "Count Your Blessings," *Sing to the Lord*, 771.
6. Killinger, *Prayer: The Act of Being with God*, 58.
7. Omartian, *The Power of Praying*, 88.
8. Cleland B. McAfee, "Near to the Heart of God," *Sing to the Lord*, 621.
9. Robert J. Morgan, *Then Sings My Soul: 150 of the World's Greatest Hymn Stories* (Nashville: Thomas Nelson, 2003), 257.
10. Joseph M. Scriven, "What a Friend We Have in Jesus," *Sing to the Lord*, 625.

Chapter Seven

1. Mark Twain, *Adventures of Huckleberry Finn* (New York: Harper & Brothers, 1912)., 14.
2. ten Boom, *Each New Day*, **p. ?**
3. Killinger, *Prayer: The Act of Being with God*, 11.
4. Christenson, *What Happens When Women Pray*, 26
5. ten Boom, *Each New Day*, p.68
6. Christenson, *What Happens When Women Pray*, 62.

7. Marshall, *Adventures in Prayer*, 58.

8. Christenson, *What Happens When Women Pray*, 53-54.

9. Allen, *All Things Are Possible Through Prayer*, 9

Chapter Eight

1. Marshall, *Adventures in Prayer*, 15-16.

2. Allen, *All Things Are Possible Through Prayer*, 8.

3. Marshall, *Adventures in Prayer*, 13.

4. Ibid., 15.

5. ten Boom, *Each New Day*, 134.

6. Ibid.

7. Marshall, *Adventures in Prayer*, 19-20.

8. Killinger, *Prayer: The Act of Being with God*, 65.

9. ten Boom, *Each New Day*, 48.

10. Marshall, *Adventures in Prayer*, 24.